Bittle en'T'ing'

ALSO BY VIRGINIA MIXSON GERATY:

A Gullah Version of *Porgy*
(the play by Dorothy and DuBose Heyward)

Maum Chrish' Chas'stun

Gulluh Fuh Oonuh (Gullah For You)
A Guide to the Gullah Language

Gullah Night Before Christmas

Bittle en'T'ing'

Gullah Cooking *with* Maum Chrish'

Virginia Mixson Geraty

SANDLAPPER PUBLISHING CO., INC.
ORANGEBURG, SOUTH CAROLINA 29115

F. Amaz. 8/10   12.95

© 1992 Virginia Mixson Geraty

Illustrations by Thomas M. Hicks, Jr.

Published by Sandlapper Publishing Co., Inc.
Orangeburg, South Carolina

MANUFACTURED IN THE UNITED STATES OF AMERICA
ISBN 0-87844-107-7

Fifth Printing, 2004

Library of Congress Cataloging in Publication Data

Geraty, Virginia Mixson.
  Bittle en' t'ing' : Gullah cooking with Maum Chrish' / Virginia Mixson Geraty.
     p.   cm.
  English and Gullah.
  ISBN 0-87844-107-7   ISBN 0-87844-110-7
  1. Cookery, American—Southern style. 2. Cookery—South Carolina.
I. Title TX715.2.S68G47 1992   91-26004
641.59757—dc20   CIP

To Dr. James G. Ward, Jr.,
who supports me in my effort,
and contributes his invaluable time and knowledge
to the preservation of our mutual love,
the Gullah language

Preface

Maum Chrish', Charleston's oldest Gullah voice, is often heard to comment in her own fascinating language on the "gwinin' en' gwinin'," meaning "the goings on," in Charleston. Sometimes positively, sometimes negatively, but usually "'e jis' onrabble 'e mout'," meaning "to comment on or to gossip."

The Maum Chrish' who shares with you her receipts for *Bittle 'en T'ing'* is fictitious; however, the Maum Chrish' who was the inspiration for this character was very much alive for about eighty-five years. "Maum," the granddaughter of a slave, lived in Saint Paul's Parish, near Charleston, South Carolina. She was born on Christmas Day and after the custom of her Yoruba ancestors, she was given that dayname.

Every Monday morning without fail, unless it was raining, Maum Chrish' was at my grandmother's house to wash and iron clothes. At that time, washing clothes was a lengthy process. An iron wash pot was filled with water, which was pumped by hand from the well into buckets. The buckets were carried to the wash pot. Wood was chopped to feed the fire that would, eventually, heat the water to boil the clothes. After the clothes were boiled in the water, which contained "Gold Dust," one of the very first powdered soaps . . . I remember it well, and the picture that decorated the box: two little black children dressed in yellow skirts . . . Maum Chrish' would "wrench" the clothes through three waters which, again, were pumped and toted to fill the three washtubs holding twenty gallons each. The final "wrench" contained "blu'n'," a liquid evidently made from indigo, which Maum added to the water to bleach the white clothes, towels, sheets, and tablecloths. These were washed first and hung on the clothesline to dry.

During this time, after Maum had put the colored clothes in the pot to boil, she would tell tales of the "ole timey" or she would offer to cook something from her unique receipts for "bittle en' t'ing'." "Bittle" is the Gullah word for victuals, or food. "En' t'ing' " means "other things."

Maum Chrish' explains in the Introduction that Mis' Ginia asked her to write down her receipts to make a book, so that future generations could enjoy the food that she cooked. Maum says she can't understand why white people need a book in order to cook. Her mother, who taught her to cook when she was just a little girl, didn't have a cookbook, and she didn't show her how to write; she only showed her how to cook.

Very well then . . .

She told Mis' Ginia to get a pencil and paper, and to write while she told her how the victuals were cooked.

Maum's inherent knowledge of her subject, explained in her charming Gullah idiom, together with her comments and innuendos, have produced an entertaining and informative "book fuh cook."

My primary purpose in publishing *Bittle en' T'ing'*, and in all my work with Gullah, is to increase public awareness of the language and to generate more interest in the preservation of this unique linguistic contribution to our American heritage which was made by the African-American people. I hope that you will enjoy *Bittle en' T'ing'* as much as I have enjoyed preparing it.

Contents

Introduction

Mis' Ginia ax'me mus' please set down dese t'ing', wuh 'e call receet, fuh mek book so all de chillun, dem, kin know huffuh cook bittle samelukkuh Uh duh cook 'um. Uh cyan' figguh huccome buckruh need book fuh cook.

Mama laa'n me fuh cook mos' sence de day Uh bin bawn. Mama yent hab no book, en' 'e yent laa'n me huffah set'um down . . . 'e jis' laa'n me huffah do.

Berrywellden, Uh tell Mis' Ginia mus' tek 'e spensul, papuh, en' t'ing' en' set 'um down sametime Uh duh onrabble me mout'.

En' 'e stan' so!

Maum Chrish'

1

1

Bittle fuh Tas'e 'e Mout'

Food to Put a Good Taste in the Mouth: Appetizers

Wash Day Soup

Dis soup berry good fuh mek on Munday, 'kase oonuh kin pit on de soup pot uhlly een de mawnin' 'fo' time fuh wash de clo'es, en' set'um back fuh cook 'tell de w'ite clo'es ready fuh heng.

Nyuse uh laa'ge bone wid 'nuf meat fuh staa't de soup, en' bil'um een uh big pot half full'up wid watuh.

W'en de w'ite clo'es done heng, 'ten' de pot. Tek all de lef' obuh wegitubble en' pit'um 'long de soupbone en' set'um back fuh cook 'tell de daa'k clo'es ready fuh heng, en' oonuh hab time fuh finish de soup.

W'en de daa'k clo'es done heng, chunk-up 'nuf I'sh 'tettuh en' pit'um een de soup pot. T'row some salt en' peppuh 'cross'um, en' set'um back fuh cook 'tell suppuh time. Mek sho' en' don' nyuse Tek-Salt 'stidduh pot-salt fuh seaz'nin'. Uh 'membuh dat time Ma graff de Tek-Salt 'stidduh de pot-salt! De soup tas'e berry po'ly, en' all ub we eenjy uh berry oncomfuhtubble night res'.

Dis saa'b 'nuf head, 'pen'pun hummuch 'tettuh gone een de pot.

Maum says:

This is very good soup to make on Monday, because you can put the soup bone on to cook early in the morning before time to wash the clothes.

To start the soup, use a large meaty bone and boil it in a big pot half full of water.

When the white clothes have been washed, rinsed, and hung on the clothesline to dry, tend the soup. Take all the leftover vegetables and put

them in the pot with the soup bone. Put the pot on the back of the range to cook slowly until you have washed, rinsed, and hung the dark clothes to dry. Then you have time to finish the soup.

Cut up enough Irish potatoes so that there is one for each person to be served, and put them into the soup. Season the pot with pepper and salt. Don't make a mistake and use Tek-Salt (Epson salt) instead of "pot salt" (table salt) to season the soup. Maum's mother made this mistake once. The soup tasted very bad and nobody slept that night.

The number of people this will serve depends on the number of potatoes that went into the soup.

Ham Bone Soup

Mus' don' t'row'way de ham bone w'en oonuh done nyam de meat. De bone stillyet hab supshun een'um.

Fuh mek de soup, pit de bone een uh pot en' kibbuhr'um wid watuh. W'en de pot staa't fuh bile, t'row een some cabbidge, en' odduh wegitubble. Seaz'n'um en' kibbuh de pot. Set'um back fuh cook 'tell suppuh time come. De mo' longuh 'e cook, de mo' bettuh 'e tas'e.

W'en de sun lean fuh down, staa't de cawnbread fuh nyam 'long de soup. Den suppuh gwi' ready w'en de mens, dem, knock-off.

Bideout de cawnbread, de soup ent specify berrywell. Wid two laa'ge cawnbread, oonuh kin saa'b ait head.

Maum says:

Don't throw away the ham bone when the meat is eaten. The bone still has much nourishment in it.

To make soup, put the bone in a pot and cover it with water. When the water starts to boil, add some cabbage, potatoes, onions, and any other vegetable you happen to have. Season the soup and set it back to cook until supper time. The longer it cooks, the better it will taste.

Just before sundown, make the cornbread so it will be ready to eat with the soup when the men and the other workers come home from the fields.

Without the cornbread this soup is a poor meal. With two large pans of cornbread, however, it will serve eight.

Okry Soup (Okra Soup)

W'en noon bell ring, pit on de soup.

Tek:

6 han' ub okry	12 medjuh ub watuh
6 laa'ge tummatuh	2 leetle spoon ub salt
3 medjum onyun	½ leetle spoon ub black peppuh
6 yeah ub cawn	1 soup bone
6 pot-spoon ub bakin greese	

Bile de soup bone een de watuh 'tell de bone t'un loose de meat. Sametime cut de cawn off'uh de cawncob; chop up de onyun en'de tummatuh, en' pit dese t'ing' 'long de soup.

T'row some salt en' peppuh en' de bakin greese 'cross'um, en' set'um back 'tell ebenin'.

Cook 'nuf rice fuh nyam 'long de soup. Dis 'nuf fuh feed twelbe head.

Maum says:

At twelve o'clock put the soup on to cook, so it will be ready for the evening meal.

Take:

6 handfuls of okra	12 cups of water
6 large tomatoes	2 teaspoons of salt
3 medium onions	½ teaspoon of black pepper
6 ears of corn	1 soup bone
12 tablespoons of bacon grease	

Boil the soup bone in the water until the meat starts to come away from the bone. Cut the corn off the corncob; chop up the onions and the tomatoes and put these in the soup.

Add the salt, pepper, and bacon grease, and set the soup back on the range to cook slowly until time for the evening meal.

Cook plenty of rice to eat with the soup. This will serve twelve.

Rooty-Baiguh Soup (Rutabaga Soup)

Mus' sho' en' mek dis soup soon attuh hog killin', w'en oonuh hab fresh hog foot fuh seaz'nin'. Nyuse de two foot fuh mek de soup. Sabe de odduhres' fuh cook 'long cabbidge en' collud green.

'Low uh medjuh ub watuh fuh eb'ry head en' bile de two hog foot een'um. Sametime chop up:

2 laa'ge rooty-baiguh tu'nip	de tu'nip green
1 medjum onyun	salt en' black peppuh

Attuh de hog foot staa't fuh bile, pit de tu'nip, de onyun, en' de green een de pot. T'row some salt en' black peppuh 'cross'um, en' cook'um 'tell de hog foot done. W'en de foot done, tek'um out de pot en' sabe'um fuh de ole mens nyam'um fuh dem hab strengk fuh wu'k.

Mash up de rooty-baiguh en' leh'um cook 'tell suppuh time.

Cawnbread mo' bettuh den rice fuh nyam' long rooty-baiguh soup. De head wuh kin eat 'pen'pun de medjuh ub watuh.

Maum says:

Be sure to make this soup soon after a hog is butchered, when you have fresh pig feet to season it. The fresh pig feet will really give it a good taste. Use two feet to season the soup. Save the other two to season cabbage or collard greens.

Allow one cup of water for each person to be served, and add the hog feet. When the feet start to boil, add:

2 large rutabaga turnips (chopped)	greens from the turnips (chopped)
1 large onion (chopped)	salt and pepper

When the hog feet are done, take them out of the soup and save them to serve to the older men to give them added strength to work.

Mash up the turnips and put them back to cook slowly until supper time.

Cornbread is better than rice to eat with rutabaga soup. The number of cups of water used will determine the number of people this receipt will feed.

Kittywah Conk Soup
(Kiawah Conch Soup)

Oonuh haffuh gone down tuh de salt fuh git conk. Fetch home 'bout twelbe conk fuh de fambly. Fetch'um een uh tub wid 'nuf salt watuh fuh kibbuhr'um, so dey ent fuh dead. Dead conk ent wut'!

Bus' de conk shell wid uh yaa'd ax eeduhso uh hatchitch, en' tek out de conk, en' chop'um up.

Tek:

de conk	1 han' ub chop onyun
2 han' ub smoke side	2 pot-spoon ub bakin greese

Cook de conk, de smoke side, en' de onyun een de bakin greese 'tell de onyun browng.

Nex' git uh laa'ge pot en' pit de conk en' t'ing' een'um. Pit 'long'um six medjuh ub watuh en' uh two quawt jaa' ub tummatuh. Seaz'n 'um wid bush en' t'ing', t'row some pot-salt 'cross'um, en' cook'um 'tell eb'ryt'ing done marriage-up.

Sabe de conk shell fuh mek paa't, eeduhso fuh maa'k grabe.

Dis mek 'nuf fuh uh laa'ge fambly.

Maum says:

You have to go down to the ocean to get conchs. Bring home about a dozen conchs for a family. Bring them in a bucket in enough saltwater to cover them, so they won't die. Dead conchs are no good.

Break the conch shells with an ax or a hatchet, and take out the conch meat. Cut the meat into small pieces.

Take:

the conch meat	1 handful of chopped onion
2 handfuls of smoked side meat	4 tablespoons of bacon drippings

Cook the conch, the smoked meat, and the onion in the bacon drippings until the onions are brown.

Next, put these things into a large pot with six cups of water and a two-quart jar of tomatoes. (Two large cans will do.) Season the soup with sage, thyme, and so on. Add some salt, and cook until everything is well blended and well done.

Save the conch shells to line paths or to adorn graves. See chapter 5, Grabe Maa'k (Marking Graves).

This will make enough soup for a large family.

Oshtuh Soup (Oyster Soup)

W'en 'e low tide, bog de maa'sh fuh de oshtuh. Den oonuh kin fin' dem "Ole Rusty" wid 'e wife on 'e back. Wrench de mud off de oshtuh 'fo' 'e op'n.

Tek:

1 medjuh oshtuh	4 medjuh ub milk
2 laa'ge spoon ub buttuh	salt en' peppuh

Cook de oshtuh een de buttuh 'tell de oshtuh staa't fuh swibble. Sametime hot de milk een uh nex' pot, 'tell de milk staa't fuh bile. Den stuhr de hot milk een de oshtuh. Mek sho' en' don' stuhr raw oshtuh een de milk. Bekasew'y de milk gwi' cuddle en' ractify de soup.

Saa'b some dem leetle oshtuh-rat cracker wid de soup. Dis kin saa'b fo' eeduhso six ef dey ent dat hongry.

Maum says:

When the tide is low, bog the marsh for the oysters. That is when you can get the old "rusty" oysters, the single ones with their wives on their backs. Rinse the mud off the oysters before you open them.

Take:

1 cup of oysters	4 cups of milk
2 tablespoons of butter	salt and pepper

Cook the oysters in the butter until the oysters begin to curl. In another pot, heat the milk until it starts to boil. When the milk begins to boil, stir it into the oysters. Never stir raw oysters into hot milk, because the milk will curdle and the soup will be ruined.

This will serve four, or six if they are not very hungry. Serve oysterettes with the soup.

Chickin Soup

Nyuse de ole roostuh, eeduhso de rumpletail fowl fuh mek chickin soup. Dey stan' so oagly de hen nebbuh pay'um no min'; dey ent able fuh specify tuh de yaa'd noway.

Wring de chickin neck en' t'row'um down fuh flap. W'en 'e done t'ru flap, scal'um, pick'um, swinge'um, en' clean'um good-fashi'n.

Nex', pit'um een uh laa'ge pot en' kibbuhr'um wid watuh. Den, chop up:
    3 laa'ge onyun
    1 bunch ub salary

Pit dese t'ing' een de pot wid de chickin en' bil'um 'tell de chickin lef' 'e bone. Tek de bone out de pot, salt'um, stuhr'um, en' leh'um res' 'tell time fuh saa'b'um.

Chickin soup berry good fuh cyo' col', teet'ache, cascade, en' mis'ry een de jint.

Dis 'nuf fuh saa'b six head.

Maum says:

Use the old roosters or the tailless fowls to make soup, because they are so ugly the hens never pay any attention to them. They are no good in the barnyard.

Wring the chicken's neck and drop him on the ground until he dies. (He will flop around for a while.) Then scald him to loosen the feathers, pull out the feathers, singe him, and eviscerate.

Put the chicken in a large pot and cover him with water.
Chop:
    three large onions
    one bunch of celery

Put these in the pot with the chicken and boil them until the chicken meat leaves the bones. Take the bones from the pot, and season, stir, and let the soup rest until time to serve it.

Chicken soup is good to cure colds, toothache, upset stomachs, and arthritis.

Serves six.

Cootuh Soup (Tortoise Soup)

Mek'ace w'en de cootuh done ketch, chop off 'e head en' heng'um up by 'e behime foot fuh de blood dreen out. W'en 'e done dreen, bile'um 'tell de meat suffuhrate f'um de shell. Sabe de shell fuh de chillun mek mud-cake, eeduhso drum, en' sabe de cootuh watuh fuh mek de soup.

Clean de cootuh, cut up de meat en' de libbuh en' bile'um een de cootuh watuh 'tell de meat tenduh. Ole cootuh tek mo' longuh fuh tenduh den nyoung cootuh. N'mine how long 'e tek!

Chop up:
  1 medjuh onyun
  2 medjuh I'sh tettuh

Pit 'long de cootuh meat de onyun en' de 'tettuh, en' cook'um 'tell de 'tettuh done.

Ef oonuh hab de luck fuh ketch 'ooman cootuh, mek sho' en' sabe de aig. Pit de aig een de pot fuh dem cook 'fo' time fuh saa'b de soup.

'Ooman cootuh mek 'nuf soup fuh ait head.

Maum says:

As soon as the cooter (tortoise) is caught, cut off the head and hang up the cooter by the hind feet so the blood can drain. After it has drained, boil the cooter until the shell comes loose. Save the shell for the children to play with. It makes a good bowl, or a drum. Save the water to make the soup.

Clean the cooter and cut up the meat and the liver. Boil the liver and the meat in the water until the meat is tender. The older the cooter, the longer it takes to become tender. Never mind how long it takes!

Chop up:
  1 cup of onion
  2 cups of Irish potatoes

Put the onion and potatoes with the cooter meat and cook it until the potatoes are done.

If you are so lucky as to have caught a female cooter, be sure to save the eggs. Put the eggs in the pot to cook just before time to serve the soup.

A female cooter will make enough soup for eight people.

Hog Head Soup

W'en uh hog done kill, ef oonuh yent hab time fuh mek scrabble, nyuse de hog head fuh mek soup 'fo' 'e hab time fuh spile.

Clean de hog head good-fashi'n en' pit'um een uh laa'ge pot. Salt'um en' kibbuhr'um wid watuh.

Bile de hog head 'tell de head tu'n loose all de meat; den tek de head bone out de pot. Sabe de head bone fuh de chillun play "Who Dat Duh Look on Me?"

Pit 'long de meat:
   6 laa'ge I'sh tettuh
   6 laa'ge onyun (wuh done chop up)

Seaz'n'um wid Roostuh sass, bush en' t'ing', en' set'um back 'tell de wegitubble done cook.

Sametime, bake uh laa'ge hoecake, eeduhso 'nuf laa'ge baddle cake fuh nyam 'long de soup. Dis 'nuf soup fuh twelbe. Ef cump'ny come, t'row some mo' watuh een de pot.

Maum says:

When the hog is killed, if you don't have time to make scrapple, use the hog head to make soup before it spoils. (Scrapple making is a lengthy process that Maum will discuss later.)

Clean the head thoroughly and put it in a large pot with enough water to cover it and some salt.

Boil the head until the meat comes away from the bone; then take out the head bone. Save the hog head bone for the children so they can play "Who Is That Looking at Me." (See chapter 5 for this game.)

Add to the meat:
   6 large Irish potatoes
   6 large onions (chopped)

Season the soup with Worcestershire sauce, sage, thyme, and salt. Set the pot back on the range to cook until the vegetables are done.

In the meantime, bake a large hoecake, or make several large batter cakes to eat with the soup. This is enough soup for twelve. If company comes, add some water to the pot!

Swimp Cocktail (Shrimp Cocktail)

Cocktail bin berry fancy bittle wuh Mis' Ginia saa'b w'en de Bishup eeduhso de Aa'kainjul come fuh shum.

Fuh mek'um, bile some swimp en' clean'um good-fashi'n. Mek some sass wid saalut dress'n', scurry-powduh, hawss-reddish, en' ketchup. Mix'um 'tell all fo' stan' de same.

Tek dem fancy leetle glass cup en' pit 'nuf swimp een'um fuh tas'e 'e mout'. Po' some sass 'cross'um, en' pit'um een de 'friguhratuh.

Uh sure ent know huccome dey call dis "cocktail," 'kase cocktail duh roostuh rump. 'E seem berry nomannusuble fuh saa'b cocktail tuh de Bishup en' de Aa'kainjul, 'speshly w'en de Prechuh hab de fowl breas' saa'b tuhr'um.

Maum says:

Shrimp Cocktail is very fancy food that is served to the bishop and to the archbishop when they come to visit the mission church.

To make it, boil some shrimp and clean them well. Make sauce with mayonnaise, curry powder, horseradish, and catsup. Mix these ingredients until they are blended well.

Put some shrimp into each cocktail glass and pour some of the sauce over them. One cup of cleaned shrimp makes two cocktails. Store the cocktails in the refrigerator.

Maum says she doesn't know why this is called "cocktail," because cocktail is rooster rump. It seems very impolite to serve cocktail to the bishop and the archbishop, while the preacher is served chicken breast.

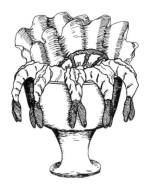

Swimp Saalut (Shrimp Salad)

Bile six medjuh ub swimp 'tell de swimp stan' pink en' de shell swink. Head'um, peel'um, clean'um, en' chop'um up.

Bile two yaa'd aig en' chop'um up. Likewise also chop up twelbe piece ub salary.

Mix'up all dese t'ing' wid uh pot-spoon ub saalut dress'n', en' seaz'n'um wid pot-salt, peppuh, en' some dat yalluh powduh wuh Mis' Ginia call "Scurry."

Pit de saalut een leetle plate wid some dem lattice leabe 'neet'um. Dis 'nuf fuh twelbe lady luncheen.

Dis de way Mis' Ginia wan' 'e swimp mix-up wid aig en' bush en' t'ing'. Mese'f redduh nyam de swimp dry 'long so. 'Co'se swimp mo' bettuh w'en 'e cook wid buttuh en' nyam wid hom'ny fuh brekwus'.

Maum says:

Boil six cups of shrimp until they are pink and the shells begin to shrink. Pull off the shrimp heads, peel off the shells, clean them, and chop them up.

Chop two hard-boiled eggs and twelve pieces of celery and add them to the shrimp. Season with salt, pepper, and curry powder, and mix with about ½ cup of mayonnaise.

On twelve salad plates put a lettuce leaf and a helping of salad. This should make enough for a luncheon for twelve ladies.

This is the way Miss Ginia wants the shrimp fixed. I'd rather eat the shrimp right from the shell. Of course, shrimp is best when it is browned in butter and eaten with grits for breakfast.

Crab Soup

Ketch two crab fuh eb'ry head. De 'ooman crab mo'bettuh den de man crab fuh mek soup, 'kase de 'ooman crab aig g'em mo' flabuh. Man crab specify berry well, en' 'e tas'e sawtuh awright, 'cep' 'e mek mo' wu'k en' trubble. Oonuh haffuh bile yaa'd aig en' nyuse de yalluh een de soup fuh tas'e 'e mout'.

Fuh mek de soup, bile de crab en' pick out de meat. Cook de crab meat en' uh laa'ge chop onyun een two laa'ge spoon ub buttuh 'tell all de buttuh done tek up.

Een uh nex' pot, hot t'ree medjuh ub milk. Stuhr one laa'ge spoon ub flowuh een de milk; den put een de crab meat en' t'ing', en' de aig. Seaz'n'um wid salt, black peppuh en' some sass een uh bottle wuh kibbuh wid browng papuh. (De name berry tangledy. Mis' Ginia call'um "Roostuh sass." Uh yent care of 'e yiz mek fuh roostuh, 'e tas'e berry good 'long de crab.)

Stuhr de pot w'ile de soup mek, eeduhso 'e gwi' skawch, en' skawch soup uh debble 'ub' uh t'ing fuh nyam. Dis mek 'nuf fuh fo'head.

Maum says:

Catch two crabs for each person to be served. The female crabs are better to make soup, because the eggs give it more flavor. Male crabs do very well but they cause more work and trouble, because you have to boil hen eggs and use the yolks in the soup to make it taste good.

To make the soup, boil the crabs (see chapter 5: How to Cook Crabs the Modern Way) and pick out the meat. Cook the crab meat and a large chopped onion in two tablespoons of butter until the butter is "taken up."

In another pot, heat three cups of milk. Stir one tablespoon of flour into the milk. Add the crab meat and the crab eggs (or one hen egg yolk). Season with salt and pepper and add some of that sauce (Worcestershire sauce) that comes in a bottle covered with brown paper. (The name is hard to pronounce. Miss Ginia calls it "Rooster sauce." I don't care if it is made for roosters, it tastes very good with crab.)

Stir the pot while the soup cooks, otherwise it will scorch and scorched soup is a devil of a thing to eat. This makes enough soup for four people.

2

Bittle fuh Greese 'e Mout'

Food to Grease the Mouth: Meats, Stews, and So On

Dress Hog   18
(Dressing a Hog)

Fry Fish   20

Chit'l'n' (Chitterlings)   20

Squayrill Stoo   21
(Squirrel Stew)

Brekwus' Swimp   22
(Breakfast Shrimp)

Maa'sh Hen   22
(Marsh Hens)

Roas' Skonk   23
(Roast Skunk)

Saa'tridge (Sausage)   24

Debble Crab   24
(Deviled Crab)

Pig Foot   26

Roas' Rokkoon   26
(Raccoon Roast)

Oshtuh Mush   27
(Oyster Mush)

Fry Chickin   28

Roas' 'Possum   29
(Opossum Roast)

Scrabble (Scrapple)   30

Swimp en' Graby   31
(Shrimp and Gravy)

Dress Hog (Dressing a Hog)

'E time fuh butchuh hog attuh de fus' fros' fall een Octobuh munt', eeduhso Nowembuh munt'. Don' wait fuh black fros'. Mus' butchuh w'en 'e col', 'cep' w'en 'e yent so col', 'cep' w'en 'e col' 'do'.

W'ile de mens, dem, kill de hog en' fetch'um tuh de yaa'd fuh dress'um, bil' uh fiah 'neet de scald'n' barril so de watuh ready fuh scal'um. Scal' de hog en' heng'um up by 'e behime foot. 'Crape de hair off de hog wid wi'ah bresh en' t'ing'.

W'en all de hair 'crape off, op'n de hog en' tek out de entrill. Gib' de entrill tuh de gal fuh dem clean'um good-fashi'n fuh mek saa'tridge. Sabe de libbuh en' de hog head fuh mek cheese, eeduhso scrabble.

Cya' de ham tuh de smokehouse en' heng'um up fuh cyo'. Likewise also heng de side een de smokehouse fuh mek smokeside.

Sabe de shoulduh fuh grin' up fuh mek saa'tridge. De fat mus' renduh fuh laa'd en' soap. De foot en' de tail sabe fuh seaz'nin' wegitubble en' t'ing'.

De hol' hog dress-out 'cep' de grunt!

Maum says:

After the first frost in October or November, it's time to butcher hogs. Don't wait for heavy frost; butcher after the weather is cold, but not freezing.

Before the men kill the hog and bring it to the house, build a fire under a barrel of water so that it is boiling hot and ready to scald it. After the hog is scalded, hang it up by the back foot, scrape the hair off with wire brushes and knives.

Cut the hog open and remove the liver and the entrails. Give the entrails to the girls to clean, turn inside out, and keep cold to make sausage. The liver and the hog head are saved to make Hog Head Cheese or Scrapple.

Carry the hams to the smokehouse to be cured. The side meat is also hung in the smokehouse.

Save the shoulders to grind up for sausage. The fat must be rendered to make lard and soap. The feet and the tail are saved to season vegetables.

The entire hog is put to use with the exception of the "grunt."

Fry Fish

Tuhreckly w'en de fish ketch, skal'um en' clean'um. Rub'um wid pot-salt en' peppuh.

Pit 'nuf laa'd een de black i'on fry pan fuh kibbuh de fish. Hot de laa'd 'tell 'e ready fuh smoke. W'ile de laa'd hot, roll de fish 'roun' een cawnmeal en' shake off dat wuh yent marriage tuhr'um.

W'en de laa'd dat hot, fry de fish 'tell alltwo de side browng.

Fry fish berry good fuh nyam 'long hom'ny, eeduhso Red Rice.

Maum says:

As soon as possible after the fish are caught, scale them and clean them. Rub them with salt and pepper inside and out.

Put enough lard or oil in a black iron frying pan to cover the fish. While the lard heats until it begins to smoke, roll the fish in cornmeal. Shake off all the meal that doesn't stick to the fish.

When the lard is very hot, fry the fish. Fry them first on one side, then turn them and fry the other side. (Fish should be turned only once.)

Fried fish is very good to eat with hominy or Red Rice.

Chit'l'n' (Chitterlings)

Sametime w'en de hog op'n en' clean out, tek de entrill en' wrench'um good-fashi'n. Tu'n de entrill inside tuh de outside en' soak'um een watuh wuh mix wid 'nuf pot-salt. Soak'um 'tell de nex' dayclean.

Nex' mawnin' dreen de entrill en' wash'um 'gen. Dreen'um 'gen en' cut'um up.

Fry de entrill en laa'd 'tell dem tu'n browng. W'en 'e browng 'e chit'l'n', en' chit'l'n' tas'e berry good fuh nyam wid hom'ny.

Maum says:

As soon as the hog is opened and cleaned out, take the entrails and clean them well. Turn them inside out and soak them overnight in salted water.

The next morning, drain the entrails and wash them again. Drain them and cut them up.

Fry them until they are brown. When they are browned, they are called "chitterlings," and they are very good to eat with hominy.

Squayrill Stoo (Squirrel Stew)

Tek cyah w'en de squayrill skin. Nail de hide up fuh dry fuh mek colluh. Sabe de tail fuh de mens weh on dem hat.

Clean de squayrill en' rub'um wid pot-salt en' peppuh. Dreedge'um wid flowuh en' browng'um een bakin greese. Sametime chop uh laa'ge onyun en' pit'um 'long de squayrill. Kibbuhr'um wid watuh, pit uh lead 'pun de pot, en' set'um back fuh cook 'tell de squayrill meat tenduh en' de graby t'ick.

One squayrill specify fuh mek stoo fuh fo' head.

Maum says:

Be careful when you skin the squirrel. Nail the hide up to dry for a collar. It makes a nice fur piece. Save the squirrel's tail for a man to wear on his hat.

Clean the squirrel and rub it with salt and pepper. Dredge it with flour and brown it in bacon drippings.

While the squirrel is browning, chop a large onion and have it ready to put in the pot. Add enough water to cover the squirrel, and add the onion. Put a lid on the pot and set it back on the range to cook until the meat is tender and the gravy is thick.

One squirrel will make enough stew for four people.

Brekwus' Swimp (Breakfast Shrimp)

If oonuh ent know huffuh cyas' net, 'e bes' buy 'e swimp f'um de swimp-man. Eeduhso 'e gwi' ju'k out 'e front buck.

Bile de swimp 'tell dey stan' red, en' dey shell swink. Head'um, peel'em en' tek out dey wane.

Hot some buttuh eeduhso some bakin greese en' cook de swimp een'em 'tell de swimp tu'n browng.

Nyam de swimp 'long hom'ny fuh brekwus'. Don' was'e de swimp 'long de chillun. Gib'um Chillun Aig en' Hom'ny. Tu'n de page fuh laa'n huffuh mek'um.

Maum says:

If you don't know how to cast a net, you had better buy your shrimp from a shrimp-man. Otherwise you will jerk out your front teeth.

Boil the shrimp until they turn pink and their shells begin to shrivel. Take off the heads, pull off the hulls, and take out the black veins.

Heat some butter or some bacon drippings and cook the shrimp in this until they are brown.

Eat the shrimp with hominy for breakfast. Don't waste any of the shrimp on the children. Give them Children's Egg and Hominy. The receipt is in the next chapter.

Maa'sh Hen (Marsh Hens)

Maa'sh hen haffuh skin, den clean out en' soak een col' watuh, pot-salt, en' uh medjuh ub wineguh 'tell dayclean eeduhso dem gwi' tas'e same lukkuh catfish.

Attuh 'e done soak 'tell dayclean, drain'um, wrench'um, en' dreedge'um wid flowuh, salt, en' peppuh; den fry'um een laa'd 'tell 'e browng.

Nex' pit uh medjuh ub watuh en' uh chop-up onyon 'long de maa'sh hen. Kibbuhr'um en' cook'um uh berry long time, eeduhso 'e yent wut'.

Cook uh laa'ge pot ub rice fuh gone 'long de maa'sh hen graby.

22

Maum says:

You have to skin marsh hens or they will have a fishy taste.

After they are skinned, clean them and soak them in cold water. Add salt and a cup of vinegar to the water and let the marsh hens soak overnight.

The next morning drain the marsh hens, rinse them, and dredge them in flour, salt, and pepper; fry them until they are browned.

Next put a cup of water and a chopped onion with the marsh hens; cover the pan, and cook them for a very long time. It takes a long time to cook marsh hens until they are tender.

Have a large pot of rice ready to eat with the marsh hen gravy.

Roas' Skonk (Roast Skunk)

Un ent nebbuh cook no skonk, fuh true. Uh ent know huffuh rid'um ub 'e smell. Uh 'membuh Gramma nyuse tuh cook'um 'do', en' 'e tas'e berry good. Gramma suh, "Attuh oonuh done skin en' clean de skonk, full uh buckut wid watuh en' stuhr six pot-spoon ub salt een'um. Pit de skonk een de watuh en' soak'um 'tell de nex' dayclean. Wrench de skonk, en' bile'um uh leetle w'ile fuh tenduhr'um. Den dreen off de watuh en' pit'um een de obun fuh roas'."

Skonk mo' bettuh fuh mek stoo. Skonk stoo tas'e berry good wid rice eeduhso cawnbread.

Maum says:

She has never cooked skunk. She doesn't know how to get rid of the smell.

She remembers that her grandmother used to cook it and it tasted very good. Her grandmother said, "After you skin and clean the skunk, fill a bucket with water and add six kitchen spoons of salt. Soak the skunk in this water until the next morning. Then take the skunk out of the salt water, rinse it, and boil it a little while to tenderize it. Then put it in the oven to roast."

Maum says it's better to make stew with the skunk. The stew is very good with rice or cornbread.

Saa'tridge (Sausage)

Oonuh cyan' mek saa'tridge sametime 'e mek chit'l'n', bekasew'y entrill haffuh nyuse fuh mek alltwo. W'en de entrill nyuse fuh saa'tridge 'e call "cas'n'."

Tek de shoulduh en' cut de meat off de bone. Grin' de shoulduh en' some de hog fat fuh tas'e e' mout'. T'row 'nuf bush en' t'ing', salt, black peppuh en' red peppuh 'cross'um en' mix'um good-fashi'n.

Full de cas'n' wid de meat. Full'um, 'cep' don' full'um so full, 'cep' full'um 'do'. Attuh de cas'n' done full, link'um en' heng'um een de smokehouse fuh cyo'.

One shoulduh kin mek 'bout fibe poun' ub saa'tridge. If enny de entrill lef' obuh, fry'um fuh chit'l'n'.

Maum says:

You can't make sausage and chitterlings at the same time because the entrails are used for both. When the entrails are used to make sausage they are called "casings."

Take a shoulder and cut the meat off the bone. Grind the meat and some of the fat to improve the taste. Add sage, thyme, salt, black pepper, and red pepper. Mix the seasonings well with the meat.

Fill the casing with the meat. Fill it full, but don't stuff it. When the casing is full, tie it into links and hang them in the smokehouse to cure.

If any of the casing is left over, fry it for chitterlings.

Debble Crab (Deviled Crab)

Bile twelbe crab, pull off de shell, en' wash'um out. Clean de crab en' t'row'way de dead man finguh. Wash de shell good-fashi'n en' set'um tuh one side. Pick out de body en' de claw meat.

Bruk'up 'nuf soduh crackuh fuh mek two medjuh en' mix um wid uh lick-up aig, salt en' peppuh.

24

Chop:
  1 piece ub salary
  1 leetle onyun
  1 pot-spoon ub green peppuh

Marriage de crab en' de soduh crackuh wid de wegitubble. Den, full de crab shell wid de mixjuh.

Melt 'nuf buttuh en' dreen'um 'cross'um fuh tas'e 'e mout'. Pit de debble crab een de obun fuh cook 'tell dem browng.

Dis 'nuf fuh feed twelbe head.

Maum says:

Boil twelve crabs, take off the shells, wash the shells, and put them aside. Clean the crabs, and be sure to discard the "dead man's fingers." (These are the dark, spongy organs in the crab that resemble fingers. It is believed that this material can cause illness or even death if eaten. Hence the name "dead man's fingers.") Pick out the meat from the body and claws.

Beat an egg and mix it with 2 cups of soda cracker crumbs. Season with salt and pepper.

Chop:
  1 piece of celery
  1 small onion
  about ¼ cup of green pepper (bell pepper)

Mix together the crab, the soda cracker mixture, and the chopped vegetables. Fill the crab shells with this mixture.

Melt some butter and pour enough over each deviled crab to give it a good taste. Put the crabs in the oven to bake until they are brown.

This will serve twelve people.

Pig Foot

Pig foot berry good fuh nyam 'long collud green.

Figguh one foot fuh eb'ry head, 'kase pig foot stan' same lukkuh cawn. Cawn ent wut' ef 'e ent nyam off'uh de yeah; pig foot ent wut' ef oonuh cyan' suggle de bone.

Clean de pig foot en' pit'um een uh pot wid 'nuf watuh fuh kibbuhr'um. T'row uh laa'ge spoon ub salt 'cross'um en' bil'um 'tell de meat staa't fuh lef' de foot. Set'um back fuh cook slow 'tell suppuh time.

Sametime cook de collud green so dem ready fuh nyam 'long de pig foot.

Maum says:

Pig feet are very good to eat with collards.

Cook one foot for each person, because pig feet are like corn on the cob. Corn isn't good unless it is eaten off the ear; pig feet are not good unless you can hold them in your hand and chew on the bones.

Clean the pig feet and put them in a pot with enough water to cover them. Add a tablespoon of salt and boil them until the meat starts to leave the bones. Put the pot back on the range to cook slowly until supper time.

At the same time, cook the collards so they are ready to eat with the pig feet.

Roas' Rokkoon (Raccoon Roast)

W'en de rokkoon done shoot, heng'um up by 'e behime foot so 'e blood kin gone tuh 'e head.

Cut off de head en' skin'um en' clean'um out. Tek cyah w'en 'e clean. Mus' cut out 'e kunnel. Mus' sho' en' don' bus' de kunnel, eeduhso de meat gwi' ractify.

Rub'um wid pot-salt en' peppuh en' browng'um een laa'd. T'row uh medjuh ub watuh 'cross'um en' pit'um een de obun fuh roas'.

Dig 'nuf swee' 'tettuh f'um de 'tettuh bank fuh eb'ry head hab two. Bake de 'tettuh 'long de rokkoon so alltwo ready fuh suppuh.

26

Maum says:

After the raccoon is shot, hang it up by the hind feet so the blood can go to its head.

Cut off the head, and skin and clean the body. Be very careful to cut out the glands under the legs. If these glands are broken, the meat will be ruined.

Rub the raccoon with salt and pepper and brown it in lard or cooking oil. Add a cup of water and put it in the oven to roast.

Dig two potatoes from the sweet potato bank for each person, and bake them along with the raccoon so they will be ready for supper.

Oshtuh Mush (Oyster Mush)

Oonuh haffuh bog de maa'sh fuh de oshtuh, eeduhso gone een 'e boat tuh de oshtuh bank.

Shuck 'nuf oshtuh fuh full uh medjuh. Sametime, bile uh medjuh ub cawnmeal een fo' medjuh ub watuh 'tell de meal spit-back.

W'en de meal spit-back, pit de oshtuh een de pot 'long'um. T'row een half uh han' ub chop onyun. Seaz'n'um wid pot-salt en' black peppuh, en' set'um back fuh cook 'tell de oshtuh done swibble.

Mus' don' was' oshtuh mush 'long de chillun. Gib' de chillun aig en' hom'ny. Dis receet mek 'nuf fuh six head ef dem ent dat hongry.

Maum says:

You have to bog the marsh for oysters or else take a boat and go to the oyster banks.

Shuck enough oysters to fill a cup. At the same time, boil a cup of cornmeal in four cups of water. Boil the meal until it "spits back" (a rapid boil).

When the meal is boiling rapidly, add the cup of oysters and about ½ cup of chopped onion. Season it with salt and pepper and cook it slowly until the edges of the oysters begin to curl. (When this occurs, the oyster mush is done.)

Children won't appreciate oyster mush. Cook eggs and hominy for them. This will feed six or eight people if they aren't too hungry.

Fry Chickin

Nyuse de fo'punce chickin fuh fry, bekasew'y leetle chickin tas'e mo' bettuh w'en 'e fry. Likewise also sabe de hen fuh lay de big yaa'd aig.

Lick-up uh aig en' uh medjuh ub milk een uh bowl. Pit uh medjuh ub flowuh en' some salt en' peppuh een uh nex' bowl.

Cut de chickin up en' drap de piece een de bowl wid de aig en' milk. Nex' roll de chickin piece 'roun' een de bowl wid de flowuh en' de salt en' peppuh, 'tell de chickin stan' so.

Hot uh medjuh ub laa'd een uh black i'on fry pan. Fry'um 'tell 'e browng good-fashi'n tuh one side, den tu'n'um obuh fuh browng tuh de odduh side.

Fry chickin berry good cump'ny wid Red Rice, eeduhso wid tettuh saalut. Uh fo'punce chickin 'nuf fuh six head, eeduhso fuh twelbe head'uh chillun.

Maum says:

Use the smaller chickens to fry, because smaller chickens taste better when fried. Also you should save the hens to lay eggs.

Beat an egg and a cup of milk in a bowl. In another bowl mix a cup of flour with salt and pepper.

Cut the chicken into serving pieces and put each piece first into the egg and milk, then into the bowl with the flour. Roll each piece in the flour until it is well coated.

Heat a cup of lard or cooking oil in a black iron frying pan. Fry the chicken until it is browned on one side; then turn it over and brown the other side. (Chicken should be turned only once!)

Fried Chicken is very good to eat with Red Rice or potato salad. One chicken should feed six adults or twelve children.

Roas' 'Possum (Opossum Roast)

Tek de dead 'possum en' pit'um een de ashish. Hol'um by 'e tail en' tu'n'um 'tell all de fuhr done bu'n off.

Tek'um out een de yaa'd en' clean'um good-fashi'n. 'Crape off de skin en' cut out de kunnul f'um 'neet' 'e two aa'm. Tek cyah en' don' bus' de kunnul en' spile de meat.

Attuh de 'possum done clean, kibbuhr'um wid watuh en' bile um fuh mek sho' 'e tenduh. Jook'um wid uh fawk eb'ry now en' den. W'en de fawk gone t'ru de meat, 'e tenduh.

Nex', dreedge de 'possum wid flowuh, pot-salt en' peppuh. Pit'um een uh pan wid 'nuf yalluh yam en' pit'um een de obun fuh roas'.

One 'possum mek 'nuf fuh saa'b fo' head. Ef oonuh hab 'nuf chillum, bes' cook two 'possum.

Maum says:

Take the dead opossum and put it in hot ashes (in the kitchen fireplace). Hold it by its tail and turn it in the ashes until all the fur is burned off.

Take it out in the yard and clean it out. Scrape all the burned fur off and very carefully take out the glands from under the arms. Don't break the glands; if you do the meat will be spoiled.

After the opossum is cleaned, cover it with water and parboil it, so that it will be tender. Stick it with a fork every once in a while. When the fork goes through the meat it is tender.

Next, dredge the opossum with flour, salt, and pepper, and put it in the oven to roast in a pan with sweet potatoes.

One opossum will serve four people. If you have a large family, you had better cook two opossums.

Scrabble (Scrapple)

Attuh de hog done dress, bile de libbuh en' de head 'tell de meat lef' de head bone. Tek out de head bone en' grin'up de meat en' de libbuh en' leh'um res' w'ile oonuh mek mush.

Bile fo' medjuh ub de pot-likkuh en' stuhr uh medjuh ub cawnmeal een'um. Cook'um 'tell all de pot-likkuh tek up.

Pit de grin'up meat en' de libbuh wid de mush en' marraige'um good-fashi'n. Seaz'n'um wid pot-salt en' peppuh. 'Pread'um out een uh flat pan fuh 'e cool.

Scrabble good fuh nyam dry' long so, eeduhso slice-up en' browng een bakin greese. Dis gwi' mek 'nuf fuh twelbe head.

Maum says:

After the hog is dressed, boil the liver and the head until the meat comes off the head bone. Grind up the meat and the liver and set it aside while you make mush.

To make mush, boil four cups of the water in which the liver and the head were cooked. Stir one cup of cornmeal into this water and cook it until all the water is absorbed.

Put the ground meat and the liver into the mush and stir until all the ingredients are well blended. Season with salt and pepper and spread the mixture out in a flat pan to cool.

You now have "scrapple," and it is good to eat just as it is or you can slice it and brown the slices in bacon drippings. This recipe should make enough for twelve servings.

Swimp en' Graby (Shrimp and Gravy)

Tek:

  2 medjuh ub swimp wuh done bin clean en' cook
  2 pot-spoon ub flowuh wuh bin mix wid salt en' peppuh
  2 pot-spoon ub bakin greese
  1 medjuh onyun wuh bin chop
  1 medjuh ub watuh

Roll de swimp 'roun' een de flowuh 'tell dem kibbuh same lukkuh de fros' done fall 'puntop'um.

Fry'um een de bakin greese 'tell dem browng.

Pit de onyun in de pan 'long de swimp en' t'row de watuh 'cross'um. Set'um back fuh cook en' mek graby fuh gone 'long wid hom'ny eeduhso cawnbread.

Dis gwi' mek 'nuf bittle fuh six head.

Maum says:

Take:

  2 cups of shrimp, cleaned and cooked
  4 tablespoons of flour, mixed with salt and pepper
  4 tablespoons of bacon drippings
  1 medium onion, chopped
  1 cup of water

Roll the shrimp around in the flour until they look as if frost has fallen on them.

Fry them in the bacon drippings until they are browned.

Put the onion in the pan with the shrimp and add the water. Set the pan back on the range to cook slowly while the gravy thickens; eat the gravy with hominy or corn bread.

This is enough for six people.

3

Bittle fuh Full 'e Mout'

Food to Fill the Mouth and Body: Vegetables,
Casseroles, and So On

Buckruh Bittle (White People's Food)

'E bin Chris'mus Day tuh de bighouse. Eb'rybody done nyam e bittle, en' de gal, dem, bin fix fuh wash dish. 'Bout dat time Jobie come tuh de kitchin. 'E done run out 'e bre't, 'e hasty tuh dat!

Uh ax'um wuh ail'um en' dis wuh 'e suh: "Maum Chrish', Ma sen' answuh! 'E suh mus' tell Mis Ray uh dog come tuh we yaa'd en' nyam us seb'npunce chickin! Ma t'row de washboa'd at'um en' 'e gone een de house en' jump 'puntop we table en' nyam all ub we dinnuh. Ma suh mus' ax Mis' Ray please kin 'e sen'um some buckruh bittle."

Mis' Ray tek uh basket en' full'um wid rice, graby, tuckry, en' t'ing'. Den 'e tell Jobie mus' cya'um tuh 'e Ma fuh dem hab merry Chris'mus.

Maum says:

It was Christmas Day. At the Rays' house everyone had finished eating and the girls were getting ready to wash the dishes when Jobie came running into the kitchen. He had been running so fast he was out of breath.

When I asked him what ailed him, he said, "Maum Chrish', I have a message from my mother. She said to tell Mrs. Ray that a dog came to our yard and ate our largest chicken. She threw the washboard at him, and then he went into the house and jumped up on the table and ate all our dinner. She said please ask Mrs. Ray if she could send her some of her food."

Mrs. Ray took a basket and filled it with rice, gravy, turkey, and other things. Then she told Jobie to take the basket to his mother so that they could have a merry Christmas.

Swimp Pullow (Shrimp Pilau)

Fry fo' slice ub side meat. Tek out de meat en' browng uh chop-up onyun een de greese. Pit two medjuh ub chop-up tummatuh 'long de onyun en' mix'um 'tell alltwo stan' so.

Pit de side meat, de onyun, en' de tummatuh een de steemuh wid uh medjuh ub rice. T'row uh medjuh ub watuh 'cross'um en' seas'n'um good-fashi'n.

W'en de rice mos' done, pit uh medjuh ub cook swimp 'long'um. Fawk'um obuh t'ree time fuh de swimp mix wid de rice.

Set'um back fuh res' 'tell dinnuh time.

Swimp Pullow good fuh hab duh wash day, w'en oonuh yent hab time fuh cook 'nuf bittle. 'E yent need nutt'n' fuh 'cump'ny'um. All de dinnuh dey dey tuh one pot.

Maum says:

Fry four slices of bacon. Take out the bacon and brown a chopped onion in the grease. Add two cups of chopped tomatoes to the onion and mix well.

Put the bacon and the onion and tomatoes in the steamer with one cup of raw rice. Add one cup of water, season and stir well.

When the rice is almost done, put a cup of cooked shrimp with it. Mix the rice and the shrimp with a fork. Set the steamer back on the range to cook slowly until time to eat.

Shrimp Pilau is good to serve on wash day when you don't have time to prepare several dishes for the meal. You don't need anything to accompany the pilau. All the dinner is there in one pot.

Hom'ny (Hominy)

Who dat ent know huffuh cook hom'ny? Lawd hab mussy! Ma laa'n me huffuh cook'um mos' sence de day Uh bin bawn.

Pit uh medjuh ub gritch een de pot 'long fibe medjuh ub watuh. T'row uh leetle spoon ub pot-salt 'cross'um.

Stuhr'um en' bile'um, en' bile'um en' stuhr'um 'tell de gritch staa't fuh spit-back.

W'en 'e staa't fuh spit-back, kibbuhr'um en' set'um back fuh cook en' res' 'tell de gritch done tek-up all de watuh. De mo' longuh 'e cook de mo' bettuh 'e tas'e.

Hom'ny good fuh nyam 'long meat, fish, swimp, en' t'ing'. 'E stan' berry well dry'long so, 'cep' some graby mek'um mo' bettuh.

Maum says:

Who is that who doesn't know how to cook hominy? Lord have mercy! Mother taught me how to cook hominy almost as soon as I was born.

Put one cup of grits in a pot with five cups of water. Add one teaspoon of salt.

Stir the grits and cook until the water begins to boil rapidly. The grits will seem to "spit back at you."

At this point, cover the pot and set it back on the range to cook slowly until all the water is taken up by the grits. The longer it cooks, the better it tastes.

Hominy is good with meat, fish, shrimp, and other things. It's good to eat alone, but it's better when eaten with gravy.

Bake Hom'ny

Tek:

2 medjuh ub col' hom'ny	1 laa'ge spoon ub buttuh
2 lick-up aig	some salt en' black peppuh
mos' uh medjuh ub milk	

Mash-up de hom'ny good-fashi'n, den stuhr een de milk en' de aig. Melt de buttuh en' stuhr'um een de mixjuh. T'row de salt en' peppuh 'cross'um.

Greese uh pan, en' pit de mixjuh een'um. Bake'um een uh medjum obun 'tell 'e set en' top tu'n browng. Dis 'nuf fuh ait head.

Maum says:

Take:

2 cups of cold hominy (cooked)	1 tablespoon of butter
2 beaten eggs	dash of both salt and pepper
2/3 cup of milk	

Mash the hominy thoroughly; then stir in the milk and the beaten eggs. Melt the butter and stir it into the mixture. Season with salt and pepper.

Put this mixture into a greased pan and cook it in a moderate oven (350°) until it is set and the top turns brown. This will serve eight.

Chillun Aig en' Hom'ny
(Children's Egg and Hominy)

Cook uh medjuh ub hom'ny fuh fo' head ub chillun. W'en de hom'ny done, bruk uh aig fuh eb'ry head. Stuhr up de aig en' t'row uh leetle salt 'cross'um. Pit some bakin greese een uh pan en' run de aig roun' een'um 'tell de aig done cook.

Marriage up de hom'ny en' de aig 'tell alltwo stan' so. Set'um back fuh res' 'tell de chillun dat hongry.

Gib de aig en' hom'ny tuh de po'ch chillun en' de yaa'd chillun. Lap chillun en' bed chillun haffuh 'pen'pun dem own Mammy fuh dem supshun.

Maum says:

Cook one cup of hominy for four children, and scramble the eggs (one for each child).

Stir them together and put the pot back on the range to stay hot until the children ask for food.

Give the egg and hominy to the children who are old enough to play on the porch and in the yard. Younger children will have to depend on their mothers for their nourishment.

Cawn Pudd'n' (Corn Pudding)

Pull six yeah ub cawn. Shuck'um en' cut de kunnel off.

Lick-up two aig, en' mix'um wid de cawn. Hot two medjuh ub milk en' po'um 'long de cawn en' de aig. Dreen two laa'ge spoon ub buttuh 'cross'um en' seaz'n'um wid pot-salt en' peppuh.

Greese uh pan en' po' de pudd'n' een'um. Pit de pan een de obun en' cook'um 'tell de aig en' milk done settle 'ese'f, en' de pudd'n' top tu'n browng.

Dis 'nuf fuh feed six head.

Maum says:

Pull or break six ears of corn from the stalks. Shuck the corn and cut the kernels from the ears.

Beat two eggs and mix them with the corn. Heat two cups of milk and mix it with the corn and eggs. Pour into this mixture two tablespoons of melted butter. Season with salt and pepper.

Pour the pudding into a greased pan and put the pan into the oven. Cook until the egg and milk mixture is firm and the top of the pudding is browned.

This recipe will make enough for six.

Pole Bean en' I'sh 'Tettuh
(Pole Beans and Irish Potatoes)

Soon attuh brekwus', pit two hamhock een de pot en' lef'um fuh boil easy 'tell oonuh gone duh gyaa'd'n fuh pick uh ap'un full ub pole bean. Wash de bean, 'tring'um, en' t'row'um een de pot 'long de hamhock.

Lef'um fuh cook 'tell oonuh gone duh gyaa'd'n 'gen fuh git 'tettuh. Dig 'nuf new leetle 'tettuh fuh eb'rybody hab six. Wash de 'tettuh en' lef' on de skin.

W'en de bean tenduh, pit de 'tettuh een de pot, en' leh'um cook 'tell dey done. Seaz'n'um en' set'um back fuh res' 'tell suppuh time.

Ef oonuh ent hab fresh bean en' 'tettuh, oonuh kin nyuse bean en' 'tettuh wuh come f'um de maa'kut, 'cep' dem ent gwi' specify lukkuh dem wuh come f'um de gyaa'd'n.

Maum says:

Soon after breakfast put two hamhocks in a pot and let them boil while you go to the garden and pick an apron full of pole beans. Wash the beans, string them, and put them in the pot with the hamhocks.

Let the beans and the hamhocks cook while you go to the garden again to dig the potatoes. Dig enough new, little potatoes so that each person will have six. Wash the potatoes, but leave the skins on them.

When the beans are tender, put the potatoes in the pot and let them cook with the beans until they are done also. Season with salt and pepper and place the pot back on the cooking surface to keep warm until time to eat.

If you don't have fresh vegetables, those that come from the market will do, but they won't taste as good as those from the garden.

Maum Chrish' Gumbo

Gumbo yent fuh mek wid no fry-bakin en' tummatuh wuh come f'um cyan. Ef oonuh ent hab de side-meat duh heng een 'e smoke-house, oonuh haffuh gone sto' fuh buy smoke side.

Fus' tek 'nuf chunk ub de side-meat en' fry'um 'tell 'e mos' done. Pit 'long de meat de okry en' tummatuh wuh done come f'um de gyaa'd'n'.

Salt'um good-fashi'n, t'row some watuh 'cross'um, en' cook'um 'tell suppuhtime.

Cook some rice fuh gone 'long de Gumbo. Dis 'nuf fuh feed fo'.

Maum says:

Gumbo isn't made with breakfast bacon and tomatoes that come from cans. If you don't have side-meat hanging (curing) in your smoke-house, you will have to go to the store to buy smoked side-meat.

First take plenty of the side-meat and cut it into chunks so that each person eating will have several pieces. Fry the meat until it is almost done; then add fresh okra and tomatoes (sliced).

Salt it, and add about a cup of water. Cook until supper time.

Have rice cooked to eat with the Gumbo. This serves four.

Swimp en' Rice (Shrimp and Rice)

Mis' Ginia buy one dem newfanglety pot wuh 'e call "steemuh" fuh cook 'e rice. All dese yeah uh binnuh cook'um een me ole i'on pot, 'cep' uh haffuh tek me time fuh 'cratch de rice cake out'um. Steemuh specify berrywell fuh cook en' fuh clean, alltwo.

Ef oonuh ent hab steemuh, 'e kin buy'um tuh Mistuh Jeems Condun sto' tuh King Street een de City. Hol'up right dey! Mis' Ginia say Mistuh Condun done mobe 'e sto' tuh de cuntry tuh we side de Ashley Ribbuh. Uh sho' hope 'e cya' dem steemuh 'long'um.

Fuh mek Swimp en' Rice, tek uh medjuh ub rice en' browng'um een uh pot-spoon ub bakin greese. Tek out de rice en' browng un onyun en' some green peppuh een de greese.

Den pit de rice, de onyun, de green peppuh, en' de bakin greese een de steemuh. Den pit uh medjuh ub watuh 'long'um. Head, clean, en' peel uh medjuh ub raw swimp en' pit'um een de steemuh 'long de rice. T'row some salt en' peppuh 'cross'um en' stuhr'um good-fashi'n. Full de bottum ub de steemuh pot half-full wid watuh.

Kibbuh de steemuh en' leh'um cook 'tell de rice grain suffuhrate, en' de swimp stan' pink. Mek sho' en' min' de watuh een de bottum paa't ub de pot.

Maum says:

Mis' Ginia bought a fancy new pot called a steamer to cook rice. All these years I have cooked rice in my old iron pot; however, it was hard to clean. The steamer cooks well and is also easy to clean.

If you don't have a steamer, you can buy one at Condon's store on King Street in Charleston. No! Mis' Ginia says Mister Condon has moved his store to the country, on our side of the Ashley River (Ashley Plaza Mall), but I surely hope he brings the steamers with him.

To make Rice and Shrimp, brown a cup of rice in two tablespoons of bacon drippings. Take the rice out and brown an onion (chopped) and some chopped green pepper in the same pan.

Put the rice, the onion and green pepper, and the bacon drippings in the top part of the steamer. Add a cup of water. Have ready one cup of raw, shelled and cleaned shrimp, and add them to the rice. Season this mixture with salt and black pepper and stir it well. Cover the steamer and let the

40

rice cook until the grains separate and the shrimp are pink. Be sure to watch the water in the bottom of the steamer. Don't let it boil out! This is tricky. Keep the water boiling, but watch it; if it boils too rapidly, it will boil over into the rice.

Hush Puppy

Tek:

2 medjuh ub cawn meal	1 leetle spoon ub pot-salt
2 laa'ge spoon ub flowuh	1 leetle spoon ub Elbo' soda
1 laa'ge spoon ub bakin' powduh	

Sif' dese t'ing' tuhgedduh. Lick-up uh aig en' mix'um wid two medjuh ub buttuhmilk. Pit fo' laa'ge spoon ub chop onyun 'long de aig en' de buttuhmilk. T'row een de cawnmeal, de flowuh en' t'ing', en' mix'um good-fashi'n.

Nyuse uh laa'ge spoon fuh medjuh de battuh, en' fry'um een hot laa'd 'tell dey browng en' swim tuh de top.

Maum says:

To make Hush Puppies take:

2 cups of cornmeal	1 teaspoon of table salt
2 tablespoons of flour	1 teaspoon of Elbo' soda (Arm and
1 tablespoon of baking powder	Hammer baking soda)

Sift these things together. Beat an egg and mix it with two cups of buttermilk. Put four tablespoons of chopped onion with the buttermilk and add the cornmeal, the flour, and the other things. Mix well.

Drop the batter from a tablespoon into hot cooking oil, and fry the hush puppies until they are browned and float to the top of the pot.

Mackyrony Pie (Macaroni)

Uh yeddy suh Yankee Doodle gone town fuh git mackyrony. Uh yent know ef 'e gone Chaa'stun eeduhso Sabannuh, 'cep' uh sho' glad 'e git'um!

Fuh mek pie, tek:

1 medjuh ub mackyrony	mos' uh medjuh ub shaa'p cheese
2 aig	1 leetle spoon ub must'ut
2 medjuh ub milk	pot-salt en' peppuh

Bile de mackyrony een 'nuf watuh 'tell 'e gib'; den dreen'um.

Lick-up de aig en' mix'um wid de milk. Grate 'nuf berry shaa'p cheese fuh mos' full'up uh medjuh. Marriage-up de mackyrony wid de aig, milk, cheese, en' de must'ut. Sabe some de cheese fuh dress de top. Seaz'n'um wid de salt en' peppuh, en' pit'um een de obun fuh bake 'tell de aig en' milk done settle 'ese'f en' de top tu'n browng.

Dis mek 'nuf fuh six head.

Maum says:

I heard that Yankee Doodle went to town to get macaroni. I don't know whether he went to Charleston or to Savannah, but I'm surely glad he found it.

To make Macaroni Pie, take:

1 cup of macaroni	2/3 cup of sharp cheese
2 eggs	1 teaspoon of mustard
2 cups of milk	salt and pepper

Boil the macaroni in plenty of water until it starts to soften (about ten minutes); then drain it.

Beat the eggs and mix them with the milk. Grate the cheese. Save some of the cheese to put on top of the pie, and mix the rest with the egg, milk, mustard, and salt and pepper. Stir in the macaroni and mix until all the ingredients are blended well.

Bake at 350° until the egg and milk are done and the top is brown.

This receipt should make enough for six.

Swimp Creo' (Shrimp Creole)

Tek:

2 medjuh ub swimp wuh done bin clean en' cook
½ medjuh ub chop onyun
½ medjuh ub chop salary
½ medjuh chop green peppuh
2 medjuh chop tummatuh

3 laa'ge spoon ub bakin greese
1 leetle spoon ub suguh
2 laa'ge spoon ub Roostuh sass
some pot-salt en' black peppuh

Cook de onyun en' de salary en' de green peppuh een de bakin greese 'tell dem saa'f.

Put 'long'um de tummatuh, de suguh en' de Roostuh sass. T'row some salt en' black peppuh 'cross'um en' cook'um 'tell de tummatuh done mush-up.

Drap de swimp een de pot en' cook'um 'tell dem hot fuh true.

Cook 'nuf rice fuh gone 'long de Creo'. Dis 'nuf fuh six head ef dem ent dat hongry.

Maum says:

Take:

2 cups of cleaned and cooked shrimp
½ cup of chopped onion
½ cup of chopped celery
½ cup of chopped green pepper
2 cups of chopped tomatoes

3 tablespoons of bacon drippings
1 teaspoon of sugar
2 tablespoons of Worcestershire sauce
some table salt and black pepper

Cook the onion, the celery, and the green pepper in the bacon grease until they are soft.

Add the tomatoes, the sugar, and the Worcestershire sauce. Season with salt and pepper, and cook until the tomatoes are soft.

Drop the shrimp into the pot and cook until the shrimp are heated.

Cook rice to eat with the Creole. This should feed six people unless they are very hungry.

Ok'ry en' Hom'ny (Okra and Hominy)

Dis berry good fuh feed nyoung chillun wuh ent yet fin' 'e teet'. 'E good sameso fuh feed ole people wuh loss 'e teet' en' ent gwi' fin'um!

Tek:

2 han' ub ok'ry   1 laa'ge spoon ub buttuh
1 medjuh ub gritch   some pot-salt en' some peppuh

Bile de ok'ry een one medjuh ub watuh. Sametime bile de gritch een ub nex' pot 'long fo' medjuh ub watuh, en' cook'um 'tell de hom'ny mek.

Dreen de ok'ry en' mix'um wid de hom'ny. Pit de buttuh en' de salt en' peppuh 'long'um.

Feed de nyoung chillun fus', en' tek cyah de ok'ry don' slip de hom'ny down dem t'roat 'fo' dem hab chance fuh chaw'um. Bekasew'y dem gwi' mek hebby cumplain!

Maum says:

Okra and Hominy is very good to give young children who don't yet have teeth. It is also good to give to old people who have lost their teeth.

Take:

2 handfuls of okra   1 tablespoon of butter
1 cup of grits   salt and pepper

Boil the okra in one cup of water. At the same time, add one cup of grits to four cups of boiling water and cook according to directions on the package.

Drain the okra and mix it with the hominy. Stir in the butter and season it with salt and pepper.

Feed the young children first and take care that the okra doesn't slip the hominy down their throats before they have a chance to chew. If this happens, they will be very unhappy and fretful, since they will still be hungry.

Hopp'n' John

Mus' sho' en' wu'k New Yeah Day, en' mus' sho' en' nyam Hopp'n' John. Hopp'n' John fetch de luck fuh oonuh able fuh wu'k eb'ry day ub de New Yeah.

Mus' don' fuhgit fuh soak de fiel' pea on New Yeah Ebe, so de pea hab chance fuh tek up de good luck wuh come fu'm middlenight tuh dayclean.

W'en 'e dayclean New Yeah mawn'n', tek:

1 medjuh ub fiel' pea	1 medjuh ub cook smoke side
4 medjuh ub watuh	(chop-up)
1 medjuh ub rice	1 medjum onyun (chop-up)
	1 leetle spoon ub salt

Bile de pea, de meat, en' de onyun een de watuh 'tell de pea mos' done. Sabe de pot-likkuh.

Pit de pea en' de meat en' de onyun een uh nex' pot 'long de rice, en' pit t'ree medjuh ub pot-likkuh 'cross'um. T'row de salt 'cross'um en' cook'um 'tell de rice grain suffuhrate.

Dis 'nuf fuh de fambly, en' dem gwi' hop libely eb'ry day de hole yeah long.

Maum says:

If you work on New Year's Day and eat Hopping John for dinner, you will be healthy and able to work every day of the year.

Be sure to soak the peas on New Year's Eve, because that is the time the peas "take up" the luck.

The next morning, take:

1 cup dried field peas	1 cup cooked smoked pork,
4 cups water	chopped
1 cup rice	1 medium onion, chopped
	1 teaspoon salt

Boil the peas with the onion and the meat until the peas are nearly done. Drain the peas, but save the water they were cooked in.

In another pot put the rice and the peas with the meat and onion. Add three cups of the water from the peas. Add the salt and cook until the rice is done.

This will feed a large family and keep them healthy all year.

Hoe Cake

Tek:

1 medjuh ub cawnmeal	1 leetle spoon ub suguh
½ leetle spoon ub pot-salt	bil'n' watuh

Mix de salt en' de suguh wid de cawnmeal. Stuhr een 'nuf bil'n' watuh fuh mek battuh.

Greese uh black i'on fry pan wid bakin greese. Dis 'nuf fuh two cake, so po' haf de battuh een de pan en' cook'um 'tell 'e browng. Po' de res' een de pan en' cook'um 'tell 'e browng sameso.

Nyam de hoe cake 'long muhlassis, eeduhso pot-likkuh.

Maum says:

Take:

1 cup of cornmeal	1 teaspoon of sugar
½ teaspoon of table salt	boiling water

Mix the salt and the sugar with the cornmeal. Stir in enough of the boiling water to make a batter.

Grease a cast-iron frying pan with bacon grease. This is enough batter to make two cakes, so pour half the batter in the pan, and cook it until it is brown. Remove it and pour the rest of the batter in the pan and cook it also.

Eat the hoe cake with molasses or with "pot liquor."

Wil' Sparruhgrass (Wild Asparagus)

Soonuh mawnin' saa'ch 'long de ditch bank fuh de sparruhgrass. Mus' cut de sparruhgrass 'fo' de sun-hot hab chance fuh tek-up de tase'.

Wash de sparruhgrass good-fashi'n so dat 'e yent cya' no san' tuh de pot. Bile de sparruhgrass 'tell 'e stan' saa'f. Dreen'um en' t'row some buttuh en' pot-salt 'cross'um. Mus' don' nyuse tummuch pot-salt; tummuch salt tek-up de tas' same lukkuh sun-hot.

Mis' Ginia lub fuh nyam 'e sparruhgrass 'puntop toas' bread. Uh lub fuh nyam me own dry 'long so!

Dis berry fancy bittle, en' 'e stan' berry good fuh gone 'long fry chickin en' rice. Sparruhgrass swink w'en 'e cook, so cut uh hebby han' fuh eb'ry head wuh gwi' nyam'um.

Maum says:

Look along the ditch banks for the asparagus. Cut it early in the morning, before the sun dries it out.

Wash the asparagus well so that it isn't sandy when it is cooked. Drain it, and put salt and butter on it. But don't use too much salt—that ruins it.

Miss Ginia likes to eat her asparagus on toast. Maum would rather eat it just as it is.

Asparagus is very fancy food, and it's very good to serve with fried chicken and rice. Asparagus shrinks when it is cooked, so cut a large handful for each person who will be eating.

Swimp en' Cawn (Shrimp and Corn)

Pull twelbe roas'n' yeah, en' cut 'nuf kun'ul off'um fuh mek two medjuh.

Sametime bile en' clean uh medjuh ub swimp.

Lick-up two aig en' mix'um wid ha'f uh medjuh ub milk, uh laa'ge spoon ub buttuh, uh leetle spoon ub Roostuh sass, en' some salt en' peppuh. Marriage-up de cawn en' de aig en' milk tuhgedduh wid de swimp.

Bake'um een uh medjum hot obun 'tell de aig en' de milk done settle 'ese'f, en' de top tu'n browng. Dis 'nuf fuh six head.

Maum says:

Pull a dozen ears of corn and cut off enough kernels to make two cups.

Boil and clean one cup of shrimp.

Beat two eggs and mix them with ½ cup of milk. Add one tablespoon of butter, a teaspoon of Worcestershire sauce, and some salt and pepper. Put the eggs and the milk with the corn and shrimp and mix well.

Bake in a moderate oven (350°) until the egg and milk is set and the top is browned. This recipe should serve six.

Maum Chrish' Red Rice

Fry 'nuf chunk ub smoke side.

Tek de meat out de pan en' cook two chop onyun en' six chop tummatuh een de greese. Ef oonuh yent hab ripe tummatuh, nyuse two can ub sto' tummatuh 'cep' mus' sho' en' dreen'um, en' pit uh leetle spoon ub suguh een'um.

Pit uh medjuh ub rice een uh pot en' pit de smoke side, de onyun en' de tummatuh 'puntop'um. T'row uh medjuh ub watuh 'cross'um. Salt'um good-fashi'n, stuhr'um, kibbuhr'um en' set'um back fuh cook slow 'tell de rice grain done suffuhrate.

Notus'um en' ef 'e stan' sawtuh dry 'fo' 'e done, t'row uh leetle watuh 'cross'um.

Maum says:

Fry enough "chunks" of the smoked meat so that each person will have several pieces to eat with the rice.

When the meat has been fried, take it out of the pan and cook two chopped onions and six chopped tomatoes in the grease. If you don't have ripe tomatoes, use two cans of tomatoes from the store, but be sure to drain them and add a teaspoon of sugar.

Put a cup of rice in a pot and put the meat, onion, and tomatoes on top. Add one cup of water. Salt well, stir, and set the pot on the range to cook until the rice is done and the grains stand apart.

Watch the rice and if it seems to dry out before it is done, add a little water.

Yalluh Yam (Sweet Potatoes)

Dig 'nuf yam f'um de 'tettuh bank. 'Low one fuh eb'ry head.

Bile de yam 'tell de skin swink. Peel'um en' slice'um t'in. Pit de 'tettuh slice een uh pan en' pit 'nuf buttuh 'cross'um. Kibbuhr'um good-fashi'n wid suguh, en' dus'um wid cinmamun.

Bake de 'tettuh een uh modulate obun 'tell all de suguh done tek-up, en' de cinmamun smell gone t're de house.

Mus' don'pit no watuh 'long'um! De suguh en' buttuh gwi' marriage-up fuh cook de 'tettuh en' tas'e 'e mout'.

Yalluh Yam berry good fuh nyam 'long Roas' 'Possum.

Maum says:

Dig enough yams (sweet potatoes) from the potato bank so that each person will have a good serving. Allow one potato for each person.

Boil the potatoes until the skins shrink. Then peel them and slice them into thin slices. Put the potato slices into a pan or baking dish and put plenty of butter over them. Cover the slices well with sugar, and sprinkle cinnamon over all.

Bake the potatoes in a moderate oven until the sugar cooks through the potatoes and the smell of cinnamon is in the house.

Don't add any water! The sugar and butter will make a syrup which will give the potatoes a delightful taste and appearance.

Yalluh Yam is very good to eat along with Opossum Roast.

Bile Cabbidge (Boiled Cabbage)

Cut two head ub cabbidge. Quawtuhr'um en' wash'um good-fashi'n.

Pit'um een uh laa'ge pot 'long two pig foot, en' kibbuhr'um wid watuh. T'row some pot-salt 'cross'um en' bile'um 'tell de pig foot done gib' up 'e meat.

Cook uh laa'ge cawnbread fuh nyam 'long de cabbidge. Dis 'nuf cabbidge fuh eight head.

Maum says:

Cut two heads of cabbage. Cut the heads into quarters, and wash them well.

Put the cabbage into a large pot with two pig feet. Cover them with water and add some salt. Boil until the meat on the pig feet leaves the bone.

Cook a large cornbread to eat with the cabbage. This is enough for eight.

Curly Flowuh (Cauliflower)

Uh yent hab much influmashun 'bout dishyuh newfanglety wegitubble. 'E stan' berry lukkuh cu'd wuh bin wrop-up een leabe. W'en 'e cook 'e smell berry lukkuh cabbidge.

Cut uh laa'ge curly flowuh fuh eb'ry fo' head. Pull off de green leabe, en' wash de curly flowuh. Dreen'um en' cut'um een fo' piece. Bile de curly flowuh een 'nuf watuh fuh kibbuhr'um. W'en 'e saa'f', melt some rat cheese en' po' obuhr'um.

'E tas'e sawtuh awright, 'cep' 'e cyan' specify lukkuh collud eeduhso cabbidge. Uh cyan' figguh huccome buckruh need fuh nyam flowuh, w'en 'e hab 'nuffuh hom'ny en' 'tettuh fuh full 'e mout'.

Maum says:

She doesn't have very much information on this newfangled vegetable. It looks like curd that has been wrapped in leaves. When it is cooked, it smells like cabbage.

Cut a large cauliflower for every four people who will be eating. Pull off the green leaves and wash the cauliflower. Drain it and cut it into four pieces. Cover the cauliflower with water and boil it until it is soft. Melt some cheddar cheese and pour it over the cauliflower.

It tastes all right, but it doesn't compare with collards or cabbage. Maum can't understand why the white people want to eat flowers, when they have plenty of hominy and potatoes to make a meal.

Tummatuh Sass (Tomato Sauce)

Fuh mek tummatuh sass, nyuse:

- 6 ripe tummatuh
- 1 chop onyun
- 1 pot-spoon ub plain flowuh
- 4 pot-spoon ub bakin greese
- some pot-salt en' peppuh

Cook de tummatuh en' de onyun een de bakin greese 'tell alltwo stan' de same.

Dreen off de bakin greese en' stuhr een de flowuh en' de salt en' peppuh. Pit de pot back on de range fuh cook slow 'tell suppuh time.

Tummatuh Sass berry good fuh nyam wid rice w'en dey yent no graby. Dis 'nuff fuh six head.

Maum says:

To make Tomato Sauce use:

- 6 ripe tomatoes
- 1 chopped onion
- 2 tablespoons of plain flour
- 8 tablespoons of bacon drippings
- some table salt and pepper

Cook the tomatoes and the onion in the bacon drippings until they are well blended.

Drain off the bacon drippings, and stir the flour, salt, and pepper into the tomatoes and onion. Place the pot on the back of the range to cook slowly until time for supper.

Tomato Sauce is very good to eat with rice when there is no gravy. This recipe is enough for six people.

Suckytash (Succotash)

Tek:

1 medjuh ub dry sibby bean
1 medjuh ub cawn ku'nul
2 laa'ge spoon ub buttuh

4 medjuh ub watuh
1 leetle spoon ub pot-salt
some peppuh

Bile de sibby bean een de watuh 'tell dem mos' done t'ru. Pit de cawn ku'nul een de same pot en' cook'um 'tell de bean en' de cawn alltwo saa'f'.

Dreen de pot-likkuh off'um en' pit de buttuh, de salt en' peppuh obuhr'um.

Ef oonuh yent hab fiel' cawn, nyuse can cawn ku'nul. Dreen'um 'fo' oonuh pit'um 'long de bean.

Suckytash berry good fuh nyam 'long rice eeduhso cawnbread.

Maum says:

Take:

1 cup of dried butter beans
1 cup of fresh corn cut from
  the cob
2 tablespons of butter

4 cups of water
1 teaspoon of salt
some pepper

Boil the beans in the water until they are nearly done. Drain off half the water and put the corn in the pot to cook with the beans until they are both done.

Drain off the pot-liquor, and add the butter and the salt and pepper.

If you don't have fresh corn, canned corn will do. Be sure it's whole corn, and drain off the liquid before adding it to the beans.

Succotash is very good to eat with rice or with cornbread.

Ok'ry (Okra)

Cut six han' ub nyoung ok'ry. Ole ok'ry ent wu't! Lef' some de stem on'um so 'e jaw ent fuh leak. Kibbuh de ok'ry wid watuh, en' t'row uh leetle spoon ub pot-salt 'cross'um. Bile de ok'ry 'tell 'e saa'f'. Dreen'um en' po' some buttuh eeduhso bakin greese 'puntop'um.

Nyam de ok'ry wid rice, hom'ny, eeduhso cawnbread.

Maum says:

Cut only the young okra. Old okra is hard and dry. It is no good! When you cut okra, don't cut the stem too close to the pod. If you do the juice will run out: " 'E jaw gwi' leak." Cover the okra with water and put a teaspoon of salt in. Boil the okra until it is soft. Then drain it and pour either butter or bacon drippings over it.

Eat the okra with rice, hominy, or cornbread.

Buckruh Ok'ry (White People's Okra)

Count de buckruh, en' cut one han' fuh eb'ry head. Wash de ok'ry en' cut'um een leetle slice.

Mekace en' dus'um wid flowuh so dem ent hab chance fuh leak tummuch. Seaz'n'um wid salt en' peppuh en' mekace en' fry'um een berry hot greese. Tek'um out de greese soon ez 'e tu'n browng. Tek cya' 'e yent bu'n.

Mis' Ginia lub 'e ok'ry stan'so. Uh tell'um ok'ry ent mek fuh chaw.

Maum says:

Count the number of people who will be eating and cut a handful of okra for each one. Wash the okra pods and cut them into slices.

Quickly dust them with flour, or the flavorful juices will be lost. Season with salt and pepper, and fry the slices in very hot cooking oil until they are browned. Be careful or they will burn.
Miss Ginia likes okra cooked this way. I told her okra is not supposed to be chewed.

4

Bittle fuh Sweet'n 'e Mout'
Food to Sweeten the Mouth: Desserts

Sweet Toot'

Oonuh hab uh sweet toot', enty?

Sometime ago Maum Chrish' was asked by the chairman of the **Charleston Receipts Cook Book** *committee to write an introduction to the new edition, explaining why the Gullah Language was used in the book. She was also asked to translate the expressions at the headings of each chapter into authentic Gullah.*

For instance, on page 311 of the **Charleston Receipts,** *the Gullah is written incorrectly to read, "Unnuh got de sweet toof, enty." The correct expression is, "Oonuh hab uh sweet toot', enty?" This translates into English, "You want something sweet to eat, don't you?"*

So, when you have a sweet tooth, you want "Bittle fuh Sweet'n 'E Mout'." This means "victuals to sweeten the mouth," or a dessert.

W'en uh binnuh leetle gal, Mama ent hab de time, needuhso de 'greedjunt fuh mek fancy cake, en' pie, en' t'ing' fuh sweet'n we mout'. 'E hab 'nuf trubble duh dus' 'roun' en' fin' bittle fuh full we mout'. Eb'nso, sometime duh Sunday ebenin', w'en us binnuh set 'roun' de fiah duh sing dem sperritual, Mama gone en' bake we uh gunjuh.

Maum says:

When I was a little girl, Mother had neither the time nor the ingredients to make fancy cakes, pies, and other desserts. She had trouble getting enough money to buy food so that we wouldn't be hungry. However, sometimes on Sunday evenings when we were sitting around the fire singing spirituals, Mother would go in and bake us some gingerbread.

Gunjuh (Ginger Cookies)

Tek:

½ medjuh ub laa'd
½ medjuh ub browng suguh
½ medjuh ub muhlassis
½ medjuh souh milk
½ leetle spoon ub wineguh

3 medjuh ub flowuh
½ leetle spoon ub pot-salt
2 leetle spoon ub cinmamun
2 leetle spoon ub ginjuh
1 leetle spoon ub Elbo' soda

Marriage-up de laa'd en' de suguh, den stuhr de muhlassis een'um.

Tek half de flowuh en' sif'um wid de salt, de soduh, de cinmamun, en' de ginjuh, den stuhr'um wid de laa'd, de suguh, en' de muhlassis.

Nex' mix de wineguh wid de milk. Tek de flowuh wuh lef' en' stuhr uh leetle een de mixjuh. Tek some de milk en' wineguh en' stuhr'um een. Do dis 'tell all de 'greedjunt done tek-up.

Roll de do' 'tell 'e t'in en' cut'um fuh stan' lukkuh boy chillun. Bake'um een uh medjum obun 'tell dey browng. Dis 'nuf do' fuh cut twenty-fo' cookie.

Maum says:

Take:

½ cup of shortening
½ cup of brown sugar
½ cup of molasses
½ cup of sour milk
½ teaspoon of vinegar

3 cups of flour
½ teaspoon of salt
2 teaspoons of cinnamon
2 teaspoons of ginger
1 teaspoon of baking soda

First, mix the shortening and the sugar thoroughly, then add the molasses.

Take about half of the flour and sift it with the salt, soda, and the spices. Stir the flour mixture into the shortening and molasses mixture.

Pour the milk and the vinegar together. Stir in the remainder of the flour alternately with the milk and vinegar mixture.

Roll out the dough and cut it into shapes resembling little boys. Bake them at 350° until they are brown. This is enough dough to make twenty-four cookies.

Rice Pudd'n' (Rice Pudding)

Tek:

2 medjuh ub milk	½ medjuh ub cook rice
1 pot-spoon ub buttuh	½ leetle spoon ub cinmamun
½ medjuh ub suguh	½ leetle spoon ub nutt'n'aig
4 aig	

Hot de milk en' pit een de suguh en' de buttuh.

Lick-up de aig en' stuhr'um een de milk, de suguh, en' de buttuh. Pit de rice een en' t'row de cinmamun en' de nutt'n'aig 'cross'um.

Bake de pudd'n een uh medjun hot obun 'tell 'e set en' de top browng.

Dis receet 'nuf fuh six head.

Maum says:

Take:

2 cups of milk	½ cup of cooked rice
1 tablespoon of butter	½ teaspoon of cinnamon
½ cup of sugar	½ teaspoon of nutmeg
4 eggs	

Heat the milk and add the sugar and butter.

Beat the eggs, and add them to the milk mixture, along with the rice, cinnamon, and nutmeg.

Bake the pudding in a moderate oven (350°) until it's firm and the top browns.

This receipt will make enough pudding to serve six people.

Bread Pudd'n'

Bread Pudd'n' mek same lukkuh Rice Pudd'n', 'cep' nyuse bread 'stidduh rice een'um, en' mus' sho' en' pit raisin een'um, en' t'row uh leetle spoon ub banilluh 'cross'um 'fo' 'e bake.

Mis' Ginia suh mus' mek Haa'd Sass fuh gone 'long de Bread Pudd'n'. De receet fuh Haa'd Sass dey dey tuh dis section.

Maum says:

Bread Pudding is made just as Rice Pudding is, except that you use bread instead of rice. The bread is cut or torn into bite-size pieces. Be sure to put raisins (about one cup) in Bread Pudding, and add a teaspoon of vanilla flavoring.

Miss Ginia says to make Hard Sauce to go with the Bread Pudding. The receipt is in this section.

Chillun Suguh Cookie
(Children's Sugar Cookies)

Tek:

½ medjuh ub suguh   1 medjuh ub flowuh

1 aig   1 leetle spoon ub banilluh flabuh

2 laa'ge spoon ub buttuh

Lick-up de aig; stuhr een de banilluh. Mix de suguh en' de buttuh, den pit de aig 'long'um. Mix de suguh, de buttuh, en' de aig wid de flowuh.

Roll'um out en' cut'um een leetle cookie. Bake'um een uh medjum hot obun 'tell dem browng.

Dis mek twenty-fo' leetle cookie.

Maum says:

Take:

½ cup sugar   1 cup flour

1 egg   1 teaspoon vanilla

2 tablespoons of butter

Beat the egg; add the vanilla. Mix the sugar and the butter; then add the beaten egg. Stir in the flour.

Roll out the dough and cut it into little cookies. Bake in a moderate oven (350°) until they brown.

Makes about twenty-four cookies.

Haa'd Sass (Hard Sauce)

Dishyuh de Haa'd Sass uh duh talk 'bout een de Bread Pudd'n' receet. Dis sass berry good fuh gone 'long Hongry Nott Tawt. Fuh mek'um, Tek:

8 laa'ge spoon ub buttuh	1 medjuh ub suguh
1 aig	¼ medjuh ub rum

Marriage-up de buttuh en' de suguh.

Suffuhrate de aig, en' lick-up de w'ite 'tell 'e 'tan-up. Lick-up de buttuh en' de suguh 'long de aig, sametime, dreen de rum 'cross'um berry easy.

Ef de rum done drink-up, nyuse wine fuh g'em flabuh, 'cep' de wine ent specify lukkuh de rum.

Maum says:

This is the Hard Sauce she was talking about in the Bread Pudding receipt. This is the sauce to serve with the Huguenot Tortes. To make it, take:

8 tablespoons of butter	1 cup of sugar
1 egg	¼ cup of rum

Mix the butter and the sugar thoroughly.

Separate the egg, and beat the white until it stands up in peaks. Beat the sugar and butter with the egg, adding the rum a little at a time.

If you have no rum, wine will do, but it won't taste as good without the rum flavor.

Hongry Nott Tawt (Huguenot Tortes)

Tek:

3 medjuh ub suguh	2 leetle spoon ub banilluh
3 aig	2 medjuh ub chop apple
6 laa'ge spoon ub flowuh	2 medjuh ub chop nott
4 leetle spoon ub bakin' powduh	some salt

Lick-up de aig good-fashi'n, den stuhr de suguh een de aig. Sif' de flowuh, de salt, en' de bakin' powduh tuhgedduh, en' stuhr'um easy een de aig en' suguh.

Nex' pit een de apple en' de nott, en' t'row de banilluh 'cross'um.

Rub uh laa'ge bakin' pan wid buttuh, en' bake de mixjuh een uh medjum hot obun 'tell 'e browng.

Sametime, whup-up some sweet cream fuh gone 'long de tawt.

Dis 'nuf fuh sixteen lady sweet'n 'e mout'. Juntlemun eenjy'um likewise also.

Maum says:

Take:

3 cups of sugar	2 teaspoons of vanilla
3 eggs	2 cups of chopped apples
6 tablespoons of flour	2 cups of chopped pecans
4 teaspoons of baking powder	some salt

Beat the eggs well; then stir in the sugar. Sift the flour, the salt, and the baking powder together and fold this mixture into the egg and sugar.

Next, stir in the apples and the nuts, and add the vanilla. Butter a large pan and bake the mixture in a moderate oven until it's done, that is, brown and crusty.

While the torte is baking, whip some cream to eat with it.

This will make enough dessert for sixteen ladies. Gentlemen enjoy it too.

Watuhmilyun (Watermelon)

Pun'kin Pie (Pumpkin Pie)

Pun'kin Pie mek same lukkuh Sweet 'Tettuh Pie 'cep' mus' sho' en' nyuse browng suguh stidduh w'ite suguh.

Bile 'nuf pun'kin fuh mek two medjuh. W'en 'e done, mix'um wid two medjuh ub browng suguh.

Lick-up two aig en' mix'um wid two medjuh ub milk. T'row de seaz'nin' een'um, en' six laa'ge spoon ub buttuh.

Po'um een two pie crus' en' bake'um een uh medjum hot obun 'tell 'e done.

Maum says:

Pumpkin Pie is made just as Sweet Potato Pie is, except that brown sugar is used instead of white sugar.

Boil enough pumpkin to make two cups. When it is done, mix it with two cups of brown sugar.

Beat two eggs and mix them with two cups of milk. Add the seasonings and six tablespoons of melted butter.

Pour the mixture into two pie crusts and bake in a moderate oven (350°) until the filling is set and the crust is brown.

Sweet 'Tettuh Pie (Sweet Potato Pie)

Bile t'ree medjum sweet 'tettuh 'tell dem done. Mus' don' peel de 'tettuh 'tell dey done bile. Den peel'um en' mash'um 'long one medjuh ub suguh.

Lick-up uh aig, en' mix'um wid one medjuh ub milk. Mix de aig en de milk wid de 'tettuh en' de suguh.

Seaz'n'um wid:

½ leetle spoon ub cinmamun   3 laa'ge spoon ub melt buttuh
¼ leetle spoon ub nutt'n'aig   ¼ leetle spoon ub salt
2 laa'ge spoon ub banilluh

Po' dis mixjuh een uh raw crus' en' bake'um een uh medjum hot obun 'tell 'e settle down en' tu'n browng.

Maum says:

Boil three medium-size sweet potatoes in their skins until done. Peel them and mash them with one cup of sugar.

Beat one egg and mix it with one cup of milk. Mix the egg and milk with the potato and sugar.

Season the mixture with:

½ teaspoon of cinnamon	3 tablespoons of melted butter
¼ teaspoon of nutmeg	¼ teaspoon of salt
2 tablespoons of vanilla	

Put the mixture into an unbaked pie shell and bake it in a moderate oven (350°) until the filling is set and turns brown.

Sillybub (Syllabub)

Tek:

4 medjuh ub cow cream	1 medjuh ub wine
1 medjuh ub cow milk	2 laa'ge spoon ub suguh

Lick'um tuhgedduh 'tell 'e stan' samelukkuh de foam wuh come off de wabe top down tuh de salt.

Gramma nyusetuh cya' de bowl tuh de cow en' milk'um fuh 'e foam. Uh yent trus' fuh do dat; Bossy too lub fuh swish 'e tail!

Po'um een twelbe leetle glass.

Maum says:

Take:

4 cups of cream	1 cup of white wine
1 cup of milk	2 tablespoons of sugar

Beat them together until it looks like the foam that comes off the ocean waves.

Grandma used to take the bowl to the cow and milk her directly into the bowl to get the foam; Maum doesn't trust Bossy not to switch her tail in the milk.

Pour it into twelve sherbet glasses.

Pine-Apple Muffin

Ef oonuh ent know huffuh mek cake, 'e haffuh gone sto' fuh buy dat newfanglety mix-up cake wuh come een box. De name 'puntop um suh "Pill-berry." Uh know 'bout skaw-berry en' black-berry 'cep' uh ent nebbuh yeddy 'bout no pill-berry, en' uh yent trus' um 'tell one dem lady tuh de sto' suh 'e stan' berry good 'long de muffin.

Buy de Pill-berry cake en uh laa'ge cyan ub c'ush' pine-apple.

Lick-up fo' aig en' stuhr'um een de mix-up cake.

Dreen some de watuh off de pine-apple, mus' lef' some. Stuhr de pine-apple een de cake, en' bake'um een muffin pan 'tell dem browng. Nyuse dem leetle papuh cup fuh cook'um een.

Pit ice'n' 'puntop'um w'en dey col', eeduhso nyam'um dry 'long so!

Maum says:

If you don't know how to make a cake, you will have to go to the store to buy that newfangled cake mix that comes in a box. The name on the box says Pillsbury. I know about strawberries and blackberries, but I have never heard of pillberries, and I didn't trust them until a lady in the store said the mix was very good to make muffins.

Buy the cake mix and a large can of crushed pineapple.

Beat four eggs and stir them into the cake mix.

Drain some of the liquid off the pineapple, but leave some of it. Stir the pineapple into the cake and, using little paper cups, bake the mix in muffin pans until the muffins are brown (using directions on the package).

Either ice the muffins or eat them just as they are.

5

Brawtus
A Little Extra

Huffuh Cook Crab Newfanglety
(How to Cook Crabs the Modern Way)

Gramma tell me, suh, "Crab lub fuh dance een de pot. Ef dem ent dance, dem ent wu't. Ef oonuh yent shum duh dance, dem done fuh dead! Mus' don' cook dead crab, 'kase ef 'e dead een de sunhot, 'e done fuh spile."

Fuh true, me ole people nyusetuh kibbuh crab wid ribbuh watuh fuh fetch'um home, den 'e stillyet 'libe w'en 'e gone een de pot. W'en dem git home, dey bile watuh en' drap de po' creetuh een'um. De crab dance, fuh true, en' 'cla'tuh Gawd dem uh debble 'ub'uh t'ing fuh smell.

Mis' Ginia suh de crab smell stan'so 'kase de crab ent bin clean out 'fo' 'e cook. Mis' Ginia ent wan' 'e house smell-up, en' 'e tell me mus' fix de crab newfanglety.

Tek uh shaa'pe knife en' jook de crab een 'e onduhside weh 'e body suffuhrate. 'E claw drap, en' 'e dead! Pull off 'e ap'un en' wrench out de body 'tell'e clean. Pit de clean crab een bil'n' watuh en' cook'um 'tell de shell red en' de meat w'ite.

Saa'b'um dry'long'so, eeduhso, pick out de meat en' mek Debble Crab.

Maum says:

Her Grandmother told her that crabs like to "dance" in the pot. If you don't see them moving, they have already died. Don't cook dead crabs, because once they are dead they spoil very rapidly.

Truly, the old people used to cover the crabs with water so they wouldn't die before they could cook them. When they got home, they would boil water and drop the live crabs in. The crabs really danced, and they were a "devil of a thing" to smell.

Miss Ginia said the crabs smelled so bad because they weren't cleaned before they were cooked. Miss Ginia didn't want her house to smell bad, and she asked me to fix the crabs the modern way.

Take a sharp knife and pierce the crab in the underbody at the point where the "apron" joins the body. The claws will relax immediately, and the crab is dead. Pull off the apron, and rinse out the material in the body cavity. Put the cleaned crab into boiling water and cook it until the shell turns red and the meat is firm and white.

Serve crabs directly from the pot, or pick out the meat to make Deviled Crab.

Grabe Maa'k (Decorations for Graves)

Oshtuh shell, conk shell, en' putty bottle specify berry well fuh maa'k grabe.

W'en de grabe done maa'k en' de du't lebble off, pit de man eeduhso de 'ooman cheer 'puntop de grabe, so dem kin res'. Likewise also, pit 'e pipe en't'ing dey dey fuh 'e cunweenyunt, en dem ent hab 'scuse fuh gone back een de house fuh git'um.

Maum says:

Oyster shells, conch shells, and pretty bottles do very well to outline and decorate graves.

When the grave is marked and the dirt leveled off, put the man's or woman's chair on the grave so that he or she can rest comfortably. Also put on the grave the person's pipe, glasses, teeth, medicine, or anything else that he or she might need. Then the person will have no excuse to come wandering back in the house.

Faa'm Bell (The Farm Bell)

Bill Browng bin de lot-man, en' 'e nyusetuh ring de faa'm bell fo' time eb'ry day.

Fus' w'en 'e dayclean duh mawnin', fuh we know 'e time fuh staa't wu'k.

De bell ring 'gen fuh noon res'. All de han' set 'roun' en' mek fiah fuh hot we dinnuh buckut. Attuh us nyam we bittle, us leddown 'neet' de tree fuh res' en' smoke pipe 'tell de nex' bell ring. Den us gone back tuh wu'k.

W'en de sun lean fuh down, Bill ring de bell fuh us knock-off. De 'ooman en' de gal gone tuh 'e house. De mens, dem, haffuh lead de mule tuh de lot fus', fuh Bill feed-up en' rack-off. Den 'e gone home fuh tek 'e res'.

Dey bin two mo' time w'en de bell ring. Ef dey bin trubble tuh de bighouse—somebody dead, eeduhso uh baby bawn. De odduh time de bell ring bin Chris'mus Ebe, w'en 'e time fuh gone Mass.

On the farm the workers' lives revolved around the farm bell, which was located at the barn, or lot, where the farm animals were kept.

Maum says:

Bill Brown was the lot-man and he would ring the bell four times each day.

First, in the morning at sunrise to let the hands know it was time to go to work.

Again at noon when it was time to rest and eat. The hands would build a little fire to heat their dinner. After they had eaten, they would rest and smoke their pipes under the trees until the bell rang for them to go back to work.

At sundown, the bell was rung again to stop work. The women and girls would go home, but the men had to lead the mules back to the barn first. Bill would then feed the animals and fill the hayracks before his long day was done.

There were two other times when the bell was rung: if there was trouble at the plantation owner's house—a death, or a birth—and on Christmas Eve when it was time to go to midnight Mass.

Who Dat Duh Look on Me?
(Who Is That Looking at Me?)

W'en all de meat gone f'um de hog head, gib de bone tuh de chillun fuh dem play game.

Dis de way 'e play:
Maa'k uh laa'ge sukkle 'puntop de groun'.
Pit de head bone een de middle.
All de chillun, dem, stan' 'roun' de aige ub de sukkle.
One chile stan' tuh de middle git on 'e two knee en' tell de bone 'e gwi' ge'm name fuh somebody wuh dead. Den, 'e ge'm de name easy so de odduh chillun ent yeddy'um. Den de chile jump up en' holluh "Who dat duh look on me?"
All de chillun try fuh guess who 'e yiz: "You Gramma? You Grampa?" W'en somebody call'um right, de chile lef' de head bone en' try fuh ketch'um. W'en 'e ketch, dat chile stan' 'long de head bone, ge'm name, en' call out "Who dat duh look on me?".
De las' one wuh git ketch, haffuh tote de hog head bone home.

Maum says:

When all the meat is eaten from the hog head, give the bone to the children to play Who Dat Duh Look on Me?

This is how the game is played:
Draw a large circle on the ground.
Put the bone in the middle.
One child stands in the middle with the bone.
The others stand around the circle.
The child in the middle stoops down and pretends to tell the head bone that he or she is giving it the name of somebody who has died. Then the child jumps up and calls out, "Who is that looking at me?"
All the other children try to guess the name the child has given the bone.
When the name is guessed, the one in the middle goes outside the circle and runs to catch the child who has guessed correctly.
The two children exchange places, and the game continues until all have had a turn.
The last child in the circle has to carry the head bone home.

W'en Uh Bin uh Little Gal
(When I Was a Little Girl)

Me min' run-on de time wuh gone,
De time w'en uh bin little.

Uh set tuh de do'step duh ebenin' time.
Set dey en' nyam me bittle.

De ole folks 'roun' de fiah
Binnuh sing dat sperritual chune.

De smoke dat dribe de skeetuh 'way
Sen' quile tuh de moon.

Den, jis' 'fo' uh drap 'sleep,
Ma cya' me tuh me bed.

Uh 'membuh yeddy'um pray tuh Gawd
Wid 'e han' 'puntop me head . . .

"Please, Gawd, watch obuh dis chile
En' keep'um nigh tuh You."

Gawd yeddy 'e pray,
En' 'E still dey dey
Duh watch en' he'p me t'ru'.

A LITTLE EXTRA

Maum says:

I'm thinking about a time long ago,
A time when I was little.

I would sit on the doorstep in the evening,
Sit there and eat my victuals.

The old folks would sit around the fire
And sing spirituals.

The smoke would drive away the mosquitoes
And send coils up to the moon.

Then just before I'd fall asleep,
Mother would carry me to my bed.

I remember hearing her pray to God,
With her hand upon my head . . .

"Please, God, watch over this child,
And keep her close to You."

God heard her prayer,
And He is still right here
To watch and help me through.

And so the sun sets on Charleston
Where the generations of the past
belong to the present, and my alter ago,
Maum Chrish', settles herself on her
doorstep and says:

"T'engk'Gawd fuh Chaa'stun"

T'engk' Gawd fuh Chaa'stun*
(Thank God for Charleston)

'E, fus daa'k en' un tek me pen een han' fuh write
Dese t'ing wuh uh t'ink 'bout Chaa'stun.

Uh yent hab onduhstan' fuh write lukkuh dem buckruh write
Wuh lib tuh Brawd Skreet.

Bekase w'en de Lawd say mus' chuse de box wuh hol'
De t'ing fuh mek we libbin',

Me ole peepul chuse de hebby box wuh hol' de mo'res
En'de box hab ax en' shubble en' hoe.

De buckruh tek de leetle box wuh lef' en' 'e git
De pensul, de papuh en' de book en' t'ing.

Berrywellden, uh yent hab de wu'd fuh write 'bout Chaa'stun . . .
Me ole home, me "Holy Lan' ".

But de Lawd know me h'aa't stan' same lukkuh dem buckruh
Wuh hab 'e name 'puntop de book wuh 'e write.

De moon done rise en' de win' fetch de smell ob de maa'sh
F'um de haa'buh ob de lan' wuh uh lub'.

T'engk'Gawd fuh life en' he'lt' fuh sing 'E, praise.
T'engk'Gawd fuh uh bin bawn en' uh gwi' die een Chaa'stun.

*Received the Pegasus Award from the Poetry Society of South Carolina

A LITTLE EXTRA

Maum says:

It's twilight and I take up my pen to write
These things that I think about Charleston.

I don't have the education to write like the buckruh write
That live on Broad Street.

Because when the Lord said to choose the box that held the
Things with which to make our living

My old people chose the heavy box that held the most, and
The box held an axe, a shovel and a hoe.

That buckruh took the little box that was left and they got
The pencil, the paper, and the books and things.

Very well then, I don't have the words to write about Charleston
My old home, my "Holy Land."

But the Lord knows that my heart "stands" just like the buckruh
Who has his name on the books that he writes.

The moon has risen now, and the wind brings the smell of the marsh
From the harbor of the land that I love.

Thank God for my life and the health to sing His praises.
Thank God that I was born and that I am going to die in Charleston.

Gullah Wu'd
Glossary

aa'kainjul—archbishop

aig—egg, eggs

ait—eight

ap'un—apron

ashish—ashes

ax—asked

baddle cake—batter cake

bakin—bacon

bakin'—baking

banilluh—vanilla

bawn—born

behime—behind

berry—very

berry fancy bittle—hors d'oeuvres

bile—boil

bittle en' t'ing'—food and other
      things

bog de maa'sh—bog through marsh
      mud

brawtus—something extra

breas'—breast

brekwus'—breakfast

bresh—brush; bush

browng'um—brown it

buckruh—white people/person

buckruh okry—okra prepared as
      white people like it

bruk-up—broken

bu'd—bird

bush en' t'ing—herbs from bushes

cascade—to be actively sick

'cawch—scorch

cawn—corn

chillun—children

chunk-up—cut up; build up fire

cinmamun—cinnamon

clo'es—clothes

collud—collard

conk—conch

cook en' res'—cook very slowly

cootuh—cooter (a turtle)

'crape—scrape

crick—creek

cu'ddle—curdle

'cump'ny wid'um—to accompany it

cyaa'b—carve

cyan'—can't

cyan' specify—doesn't come up to expectations

cyo'—cure

daa'k—dark

de—the

de salt—the ocean

dese—these

dis—this

dreege—dredge

dreen—drain

dry'long so—for no particular reason; also, plain, or without decorations

dus' 'roun'—to work so fast as to stir the dust

dus'um—to cover, as with flour

ebenin'—evening

eb'ry—every

een—in

eenj'y uh berry oncumfuhtubble night res'—slept very poorly

'e jaw fuh leak—he/it is salivating

Elbo' soda—baking soda

en'—and

en' t'ing'—and other things

ent wu't—is worthless

fawk'um obuh—turn gently with fork

feed-up—feed and water farm animals

fiah—fire

figguh—figure

fin' bittle—to furnish food

flabuh—flavor

flap—contortions of beheaded fowl

'fo'—before

fo'—four

fo'punce—four pence

fowl breas'—the breast of a fowl

fry-bakin—bacon sliced for frying

fuh—for

fuhr—fur

'gen—again

gib-up 'e meat—in cooking, when meat leaves the bone

ginjuh—ginger

good-fashi'n—thoroughly

graby—gravy

graff—to grab

gunjuh—ginger bread, ginger cookies

gyaa'd'n—garden

han'—one handful; also, a farm worker

hatchitch—hatchet

hawss-reddish—horseradish

head—one person

hebby han'—generous

heng—hang

hongry—hungry

hot—heat

huccome—how come; why

I'sh 'tettuh—Irish potato

jaa'—jar

jook'um—to stick it/ him, etc.

'kase—because

kibbuhr'um—to cover it

kin—can

kitchen spoon—two tablespoons

Kittywah—Kiawah Island, S.C.

knock-off—to stop work

kunnul—kernel

laa'd—lard

laa'ge spoon—tablespoon

laa'n—taught

lap chile—child too young to sit or play on the floor

lattice—lettuce

"Lawd hab mussy"—Lord have mercy

leetle spoon—teaspoon

libbuh—liver

lick-up—to beat; beaten

link'um—form sausage links

maa'k grabe—to outline graves

marriage'um—to mix ingredients well

medjuh—a cup

medjum—medium

medjum hot obun—medium heat: 350°

mek—make

mekace—hurry

mos' uh medjuh—3/4 cup

'neet—under

newfanglety—new; modern

nex'—next; also, the other

nomannusubble—having no manners

noon res'—time when farm hands eat lunch and rest

'nuf—enough

nutt'n'aig—nutmeg

nyam—to eat

nyuse—use

oagley—ugly

obun—oven

obuhr'um—over them

odduhres'—the others; the rest

"ole Rusty"—an old crab or oyster

onkibbuh—uncover

'ooman—woman; women; female

onyun—onion

oonuh—you

oshtuh bank—an oyster bed

oshtuh-rat—oysterettes

paa't—part; also, path

pen'pun—depends upon

pick'um—remove shells from shrimp

pit—put

pledjuhr'um—to give pleasure to

po'—poor; also, pour

po'ch chile—child too young to be in the yard

po'ly—not well

pot-likkuh—pot liquor

pot-salt—sodium chloride

pot-spoon—a kitchen spoon, two tablespoons

puhwishun—provisions

'puntop—on top

quawt—quart

ractify—broken; worthless

receet—recipe

roostuh sass—Worcestershire sauce

rumpletail—a tailless fowl

saa'b—serve

saa'f—soft

saalut—salad

saa'tridge—sausage

sabe—save

salary—celery

sawtuh—sort of

scal'—scald

scurry-powduh—curry powder

seaz'nin'—seasoning

seaz'n'um—season it/them

sence—since

settle 'ese'f—become firm

sibby bean—butter bean

skreet—street

sparruh-grass—asparagus

spensul—pencil

sperritual—spiritual

spit-back—boiling grits, cornmeal

squayrill—squirrel

stan' so—is so; looks to be so

'stidduh—instead of

sto'—store

suffuhrate—separate

suggle—to suck and chew

supshun—sustenance

swibble—shrivel

swimp—shrimp

swinge'um—singe it/them, etc.

Tek-Salt—Epsom salts

'tell—until

'tell 'e done—until it is done or cooked

'ten'—attend to

tengledy—confusing

'tettuh—potato

t'ing—thing

t'ing'—things

t'ree—three

tuhreckly—directly

tummatuh—tomato

ub—of

Uh—I

uhlly—early

watuh—water

wegitubble—vegetable

w'en—when

wid—with

wineguh—vinegar

w'ite—white

wrench—rinse

wuh—what

wu'k—work

wu't—worth

yaa'd-aig—an egg laid by a hen in
the yard, not bought

yaa'd chile—a child old enough to
play outside in the yard

yalluh—yellow

yeah—ear; also, year